The English Poets of the First World War

THAMES
AND
HUDSON

JOHN LEHMANN

The English Poets of the First World War

with 58 illustrations

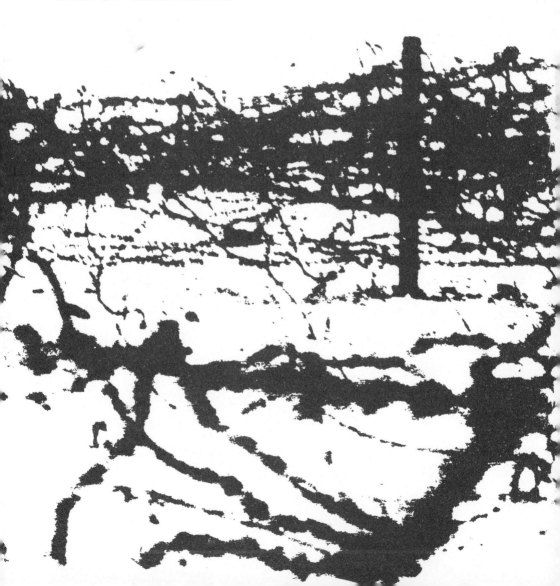

Acknowledgments

For the use of copyright material acknowledgments are due to the following: Chatto and Windus Ltd for poems by Robert Nichols from *Such Was My Singing*, 1942; Faber and Faber Ltd for extracts from *In Parenthesis* by David Jones; David Higham Associates for 'Babel' by Osbert Sitwell from *Selected Poems*, 1943, and for poems by Herbert Read from *Collected Poems*, 1963; Oxford University Press for poems by Ivor Gurney from *Selected Poems by Ivor Gurney*, 1982; A. D. Peters & Co. Ltd for poems by Edmund Blunden from *Poems 1914–30*, 1930; George Sassoon and Viking Press for poems by Siegfried Sassoon; Sidgwick & Jackson Ltd for 'Prisoners' by F. W. Harvey from *Gloucestershire Friends*, 1917; A. P. Watt & Son for poems by Robert Graves from *Fairies and Fusiliers*, 1917, and *Collected Poems 1914–1947*, 1948.

I wish to express my warmest thanks to Mrs Lola Szladits for permission to study original letters and annotated first editions in the possession of the Henry W. and Albert A. Berg Collection in the New York Public Library Astor, Lenox and Tilden Foundations, to Mr Christopher Hawtree for invaluable assistance in research and preparation of the manuscript, and to my publishers for their continual sympathy and many excellent suggestions.

Contents

THE RUPTURE.

DEPARTURE OF GERMAN AMBASSADOR.

FORMAL DECLARATION.
ST. PETERSBURG, Aug. 1.

The German Ambassador, in the name of his Government, handed to the Foreign Ministry a Declaration of War at 7.30 this evening.

The staff of the German Embassy left to-night.—Reuter.

SCENES IN ST. PETERSBURG.

ST. PETERSBURG, Aug. 1.

Stirring scenes were witnessed here to-day when the enrolling of reservists from 100 centres took place, starting from six in the morning.

Women and children were accompanying their husbands and fathers, while the priests were blessing the reservists as they went through the town singing hymns.

Great demonstrations of many thousands of people took place last night before the Admiralty and the statue of Peter the Great.

The *Novoe Vremya* in its issue last evening says that the words " hatred, mendacity, and bloodthirstiness " constitute the motto of Austria, but such a device will never lead to victory.

The following official *communiqué* has been published here :—

The continual demonstrations, in which more and more numerous crowds participate, and which take place even at night, induce the Government, which completely shares this patriotic enthusiasm, to make a fresh appeal to the population to preserve calm and self-restraint and to avoid the expression of their excited feelings, which can only complicate the present situation.—*Reuter.*

GERMAN ULTIMATUM.

THE BEGINNING OF WAR.

INVASION OF LUXEMBURG.

CONFLICT ON THE RUSSIAN FRONTIER.

BRITISH RESPONSIBILITIES.

A Reuter telegram from Luxemburg states that the German troops have entered the Grand Duchy and have seized the Government Offices, and that telephone communication has been cut.

A Reuter telegram from Berlin states that a German patrol near Gross Prostken, three hundred yards on the German side of the Russian frontier, was fired upon yesterday by a Russian frontier patrol, and that the Germans returned the fire. Neither side suffered any loss.

In virtue of the Treaty of London signed on May 11, 1867, the Grand Duchy of Luxemburg was neutralized under the collective guarantee of the signatory Powers. The signatories also bound themselves to respect its neutrality (Article II.). The signatory Powers were Great Britain, France, Russia, the Netherlands, Belgium, Italy, Prussia, and Austria-Hungary.

The invasion of Luxemburg is a violation of this Treaty, which Great Britain, in common with France, Russia, and the Netherlands is pledged to uphold.

THE DUTY OF FRANCE.

M. POINCARÉ'S PUBLIC PROCLAMATION.

ENTHUSIASM IN PARIS.

(FROM OUR OWN CORRESPONDENT.)

PARIS, Aug. 1.

The following proclamation has been issued to the people of France by President Poincaré :—

For some days the condition of Europe has become considerably more serious in spite of the efforts of diplomacy. The horizon has become darkened.

At this hour most of the Nations have mobilized their forces.

Some countries, even though protected by neutrality, have thought it right to take this step as a precaution.

Some Powers, whose constitutional and military laws do not resemble our own, have without issuing a decree of mobilization begun and continued preparations which are in reality equivalent to mobilization and which are nothing more or less than an anticipation of it (*qui n'en sont que l'exécution anticipée*).

France, who has always declared her pacific intentions, and who has at the darkest hours (*dans des heures tragiques*) given to Europe counsels of moderation and a living example of prudence (*sagesse*), who has multiplied her efforts for the maintenance of the world's peace, has herself prepared for all eventualities and has taken from this moment the first indispensable measures for the safety of her territory.

But our legislation does not allow us to complete these preparations without a decree of mobilization.

Careful of its responsibility and realizing that it would be failing in a sacred task to leave things as they were, the Government has issued the decree which the situation demands.

Mobilization is not war. In the present

On 3 August Germany declared war on France and invaded Belgium, and the British cabinet authorized the mobilization of the army. The next day George V and his privy council formally proclaimed a state of war. The whole of the British Expeditionary Force was sent to France

I

Introduction

THIS is a book about the young Englishmen who fought in the First World War and wrote poetry about their experiences, or their anticipation of such experiences. All of them were enrolled in and put on the uniform of one branch or other of the British forces, though not all of them were actually involved in fighting; Rupert Brooke, for instance, died just before he could take part in the Gallipoli landings. Some were killed, some survived the conflict to write of their experiences later as well as at the time. Such later recollections and reflections also I have thought it appropriate to consider and quote from.

The harvest of the writings of these young Englishmen was considerable, and has left a profound impact on the course of English poetry since their time. No previous war in which these islands were involved left any poetic harvest at all from the actual combatants. The main reason is clear: the First World War was the first in which ordinary educated English civilians took part, either by voluntary enlistment or later conscription. The Napoleonic Wars were fought by professional armies, as was the Crimean War. The first major modern war in which educated civilians were involved was the American Civil War; but no Englishmen were involved, or at any rate no articulate Englishmen.

There was a period, during and directly after the War, when almost any young man who could express his thoughts and feelings in verse could find a publisher and a public. Most of them have fallen out of memory, and most of them, regrettably, rightly so; though I do not put it out of the bounds of possibility that one day a rediscovery of genuine poetic talent will be made among these neglected, dusty volumes; or even that unpublished work of real significance may be found one day in a pile of forgotten and never properly examined papers of some soldier, unknown as a poet, who was killed before the Armistice of 1918.

In the event I have confined myself to a study of fifteen of the most prominent and gifted poets – and a brief mention of six minor poets – of that period who fall within my terms of reference. Many poems were written on war themes by outstanding poets of an older generation, or by other contemporaries who for one reason or another were not involved in the uniformed forces. Many of these, such as the poems by Thomas Hardy, are part of our great poetic heritage; but they do not concern me here.

*   *   *

The English poetry of the First World War can, roughly, be divided into two periods: the early period, from the outbreak of war to about 1916, the time of the Battle of the Somme; and the later period, from 1916 to 1918 and the Armistice. The two periods are very different in mood. In the earlier period the poets, like the mass of non-combatants (on both sides of the fighting lines) believed in a simple, heroic vision of a struggle for the right, of noble sacrifice for an ideal of patriotism and country. As the war dragged on, and dreams of an early conclusion to the hostilities faded, the mood changed and darkened. On the Western Front, which became the chief theatre of war, the lines of the opposing armies changed by only a few miles on either side for year after year. It became a war of attrition, in which huge offensives were planned, again and again, and failed, at a shattering cost in material and lives. The carnage and suffering were ceaseless and, to those taking part with rifle and bomb, increasingly pointless and full of horror.

The dividing point between the two periods, the two moods, came, as I have said, about 1916, during the Battle of the Somme. The outstanding poets of the first period were Julian Grenfell, Rupert Brooke and Robert Nichols; but after Beaumont Hamel and Passchendaele no one of any sensibility could write any more as they had written. The dreams were shattered, and patriotism became a matter of grim endurance against all odds, of despairing hope almost buried beneath the huge weight of disillusionment, of the need not to be defeated existing beside the belief that it was increasingly not merely stupid but almost criminal not to negotiate an end to the slaughter. The chief, but by no means isolated voices of this new mood among the poets, which brought forth what is still most memorable and enduring to later generations, were Siegfried Sassoon, Wilfred Owen, Edmund Blunden and Isaac Rosenberg.

At the same time, two phenomena made themselves increasingly apparent. The first was the growing alienation between the men fighting in France and Flanders and the civilians, both young and old, at home in Britain. Soldiers returning on leave found it almost impossible, and at times totally impossible, to make their mothers and fathers and sweethearts understand what was happening the other side of the Channel, the depth of suffering and despair that was being experienced in the trenches. Coming back from leave, many in fact welcomed the return to what was to them real existence: danger, death, mutilation and the ruined landscapes of the fighting areas.

Two separate worlds were developing: the world of make-believe at home, and the enclosed, entirely male, comfortless world of bombardment and slaughter, ruled by martial discipline and illumined only by camaraderie and heroic selflessness.

It was this intense and inevitable camaraderie that produced the second phenomenon: deep feelings developed between the fighting men, above all between the young officers and the soldiers in the platoons they commanded. This was not confined to poets such as Owen and Sassoon who did not attempt to conceal their feelings in what they wrote, and who in any case had strong homosexual impulses; it also appears in the work of poets such as Nichols, Blunden and Robert Graves, whose subsequent history makes it impossible to consider as other than basically heterosexual. As the American critic, Paul Fussell, has commented in *The Great War and Modern Memory*, this phenomenon is characteristic of both the poetry and prose of the more articulate recorders of their front-line experiences. Such a mood often develops under conditions where young males are thrown together for long periods, but the peculiar conditions of front-line warfare, when danger of death and mutilation are ever present, inevitably intensified camaraderie into something deeper and more emotional: the beautiful young man dying in the arms of his fellow soldier or officer could hardly fail to arouse feelings very close to love. Professor Fussell maintains that such feelings already had literary ancestry in the very recent past. He writes in 'Soldier Boys' of:

some of the reasons for the homo-erotic motif in Great War writings. Chief among them is the war's almost immediate proximity to such phenomena as the Aesthetic Movement, one of whose more powerful impulses was the rediscovery of the erotic attractiveness of young men. Aestheticism was an offshoot of the kind of warm late-Romanticism that makes it seem appropriate that Tennyson should be fond of Arthur Hallam, Whitman of Peter Doyle, and Housman of Moses Jackson.

Fussell ties in this view with the argument that for the educated English combatants the First World War was a very literary war. This condition, the varying situations in which they found themselves, reminded them instinctively of historical situations reflected in a long national literary tradition, often going back in fact to the Greek and Roman poets and historians whom they had studied in school and university. He concludes that 'American, French and German reminiscences of the war behave very differently'.

I have singled out these two phenomena because they are fundamental to an understanding of the English literature that was inspired by the First World War. But of course there were many other characteristics of significant relevance that will, I hope, emerge as I consider the outstanding poets individually.

2

Grenfell, Brooke, Sorley and Nichols

IT is strange that one of the most memorable of the poems written during the first phase of the war was the work of a professional soldier, Julian Grenfell, who was awarded the D.S.O. for bravery in battle. Grenfell came from an aristocratic family. Accomplished though the poem is without any doubt, he has not been known to have published or circulated any other poems. Stranger still is the fact that, unlike the great majority of the other poems written during the earlier and also the later phase of the war, it is neither a poem extolling patriotism and the need to defend the sacred shores of England against a ruthless enemy, nor an exposition of the horror and futility of modern warfare. 'Into Battle', which was written in the early months of 1915, is quite simply a hymn to the splendour of fighting and the fighting man's destiny, almost mystic in its implication. It begins:

> The naked earth is warm with Spring,
>   And with green grass and bursting trees
> Leans to the sun's gaze glorying,
>   And quivers in the sunny breeze;
>
> And life is colour and warmth and light,
>   And a striving evermore for these;

And he is dead who will not fight;
   And who dies fighting has increase.

The fighting man shall from the sun
   Take warmth, and life from the glowing earth;
Speed with the light-foot winds to run,
   And with the trees to newer birth;
And find, when fighting shall be done,
   Great rest, and fullness after dearth.

All the bright company of Heaven
   Hold him in their high comradeship,
The Dog-Star, and the Sisters Seven,
   Orion's Belt and sworded hip.

Grenfell was the elder son of Lord and Lady Desborough, whose home, Taplow Court in Buckinghamshire, had become the weekend rendezvous of distinguished politicians and intellectuals with political interests. 'Ettie' Desborough, his mother, was a well-known and popular hostess, beautiful, much courted and certainly not insensitive to the advances of her many admirers; while her husband was more interested in sport, and in particular rowing activities on the nearby Thames. She adored her two sons, Julian and Billy (both of whom were killed during the war), but from adolescence Julian showed himself increasingly a rebel against the values and the code by which his parents and their upper-class circle lived. When he was twenty-one he wrote a series of essays amplifying and arguing his views at some length. They were never published, and after his death his mother hid them at the bottom of a trunk containing his effects.

The mystic note deepens as the poem goes on, identifying, in a decidedly un-Wordsworthian way, the fighting man with nature, with trees, birds and horses which, the lines suggest, are one with him in the desire to live by continual strife and the ecstasy of joy that the crisis of fighting to exist brings with it:

The woodland trees that stand together,
  They stand to him each one a friend;
They gently speak in the windy weather;
  They guide to valley and ridge's end.

The kestrel hovering by day,
  And the little owls that call by night,
Bid him be swift and keen as they,
  As keen of ear, as swift of sight.

The blackbird sings to him, 'Brother, brother,
  If this be the last song you shall sing,
Sing well, for you may not sing another;
  Brother, sing.'

In dreary, doubtful waiting hours,
  Before the brazen frenzy starts,
The horses show him nobler powers;
  O patient eyes, courageous hearts!

The resounding conclusion of the poem is, in a sense, an exalted poetic affirmation of the fatalism which most soldiers learn to live by: 'If your number's on it, it'll get you: no use worrying.'

Through joy and blindness he shall know,
  Not caring much to know, that still
Nor lead nor steel shall reach him, so
  That it be not the Destined Will.

The thundering line of battle stands,
  And in the air Death moans and sings;
But Day shall clasp him with strong hands,
  And Night shall fold him in soft wings.

This is no Christian poem and, one must add, no specifically English poem. It could have been written as well by a brave and dedicated German, Austrian or

Russian soldier. It is scarcely possible not to see in it a symbolic and no doubt unconscious transposition of the orgasm of love. One might say that if Hotspur had written poetry, this poem would belong in an anthology with his most characteristic pieces. The critics have found it almost embarrassing to place, though they realize that its skilled felicity of utterance makes it impossible to ignore. 'It can't be done again,' said Sir Walter Raleigh on reading it (and it never was). '*Into Battle* may have little affinity with the more obvious mode of Georgian lyricism', John H. Johnston duly concludes in *English Poetry of the First World War*, 'but, like [Rupert Brooke's] *1914*, it is a specialized response and therefore embodies only limited values.'

Rupert Brooke and Julian Grenfell were born within a few months of one another and came from the same class background. While Brooke was at Cambridge he attracted the attention of Edward Marsh, a rising civil servant of modest independent means which he used to act as patron to young artists and poets. Brooke became a favourite in his circle and, as Grenfell was also a friend of Marsh's, it is not impossible that the two met at Marsh's house. Nevertheless Brooke is unlikely to have seen 'Into Battle', because Grenfell, who had joined the Royal Dragoons in 1910, appears to have written the poem in May 1915, and it was not published in *The Times* until a month after Brooke's death.

In 1907 Brooke left Rugby, where his father was a housemaster, and went up to King's College Cambridge, where he very soon distinguished himself in various spheres: he was preternaturally good-looking, he quickly became associated with the amateur dramatic activities of the university and in particular with the founding of the Marlowe Dramatic Society, became a keen supporter of the Fabians and in fact was elected president of the

Cambridge branch a year or two after joining. Ever since
his last years at Rugby he had been writing poetry, and
continued at Cambridge with renewed zest. His early
influences had been of the decadent Romanticism of the
1890s, and are all but negligible. Intellectual Cambridge,
however, was at that time in the grip of a new enthusiasm
for the metaphysical poets of the 17th century, in particular for the work of John Donne; and the new poems he
began to write show the conflict between his old influences
and the new. He never entirely lost the Romantic touch,
which crops up again and again in the poems which he
finally winnowed to make a volume: *Poems 1911*. What was
interesting, however, in this volume, apart from its fluent
accomplishment of verse-making, was a new realism. This
appeared to some of the critics of the time even crude and
shocking, though the more percipient of them were aware
that a new poet of eminence, if still confused promise, had
emerged; a young poet moreover in tune with the new
anti-romantic spirit which, in poems such as Masefield's
'Everlasting Mercy', had already made a mark.

Very soon after the appearance of *Poems 1911*, Brooke
had an unhappy love-affair, and a serious nervous breakdown as a result of it. His closest friends maintain that he
was never quite the same buoyant, well-balanced person
afterwards. Nevertheless, he was capable, between 1912
and the outbreak of war, of writing a handful of poems
which are remarkable for combining light verse and metaphysical wit with fanciful nostalgia and the happiness of
undemanding, reciprocated love. He travelled to Europe;
he wrote his famous 'The Old Vicarage, Grantchester' at
a café in Berlin; he made a long expedition to America and
Canada, during which he wrote some brilliant travel
essays. He went on to the South Seas where, in Tahiti, he
fell in love with a native girl and wrote for her one of his
most delightful and successful poems, 'Tiare Tahiti', in
his now favourite octosyllabics.

1 An early recruiting poster appealing to patriotism: by such methods 2½ million men were encouraged to enlist before conscription began in 1916

2 Julian Henry Francis Grenfell, *c.*1914

3 Rupert Brooke, the most famous poet of the early war years, in 1913

4 Charles Hamilton Sorley. Portrait by C. Jameson, 1916

5 Robert Nichols. Portrait by Augustus John, 1921

6 Rupert Brooke on a picnic with friends, *c.* 1909

7 Bayonet practice with bags of straw: Winnipeg Rifles on Salisbury Plain

8, 9 Enlistment: *above*, recruits with sergeant; *below*, recruits are fitted up with kit

10 Augustus John, *Fraternity* (undated)

It is important to emphasize this phase in his development, because its mood is in such striking contrast to the mood of the *1914 Sonnets*, his only true war poems. These were written while he was training as a soldier and before he went as a member of the Gallipoli expedition during which he died of septicaemia. After his nervous collapse in the early months of 1912, he had broken with many of his Cambridge friends, in particular Lytton Strachey and his Bloomsbury circle, and in their stead had, through the assiduous advocacy of Marsh, now Winston Churchill's secretary, found new friends among the 'top people', politicians and soldiers, who were running the war. He had also been instrumental in launching with Marsh the series of *Georgian Poetry* (first volume 1911–12) which made such a mark on the times. It seems to me highly unlikely that if he had still been in close touch with his earlier friends, with their well-known scepticism, agnosticism and distrust of romantic emotion, the *1914 Sonnets* would have taken the shape they did. Many of these friends believed that it was only a passing uncharacteristic mood that produced them, and that if he had lived his later poems would have been much more in tune with his earlier work: they nevertheless made his immediate fame and laid the foundations of an enduring legend. It all began with the Dean of St Paul's, Inge, reading out in his Easter sermon perhaps the most famous of the five poems, 'The Soldier':

If I should die, think only this of me:
That there's some corner of a foreign field
That is forever England. There shall be
In that rich earth a richer dust concealed;
A dust whom England bore, shaped, made aware,
Gave, once, her flowers to love, her ways to roam,
A body of England's, breathing English air,
Washed by the rivers, blest by suns of home.

(3)

The ~~Glorious~~ Dead.

Blow out, you bugles, over the rich Dead!
    There's none of these so lonely and poor of old
    But, dying, ~~has~~ has made us rarer gifts than gold.
These laid the world away; poured out the red
Rich wine of youth; gave up the years to be
    Of work and ~~joyous~~ joy, and that unhoped serene,
    That men call age; and those who would have been,
Their sons, they gave, their immortality.

Blow, bugles, blow! They brought us, for our dearth,
    Holiness, lacked so long, and Love, and Pain.
Honour has come back, as a king, to earth,
    And paid his subjects with a royal wage;
And nobleness walks in our ways again;
    And we have come into our heritage.

Rupert Brooke's second draft of 'The Dead', 1914

And think, this heart, all evil shed away,
A pulse in the eternal mind, no less
Gives somewhere back the thoughts by England given;
Her sights and sounds; dreams happy as her day;
And laughter, learnt of friends; and gentleness,
In hearts at peace, under an English heaven.

All the sonnets are fluent, skilful and mellifluous. They hit exactly the right note of love of his country, patriotic self-sacrifice in a noble cause, and release from the petty preoccupations of peacetime (including, it seems, love) at a moment when the country needed to find a youthful hero to embody its most idealistic dreams of a just war against ruthless enemies. When Brooke died in the Aegean, Churchill himself wrote a fulsome obituary in *The Times* which sounded exactly this note, and accelerated the growth of the Rupert Brooke legend. And yet now, after the disillusionment of the later course of the war, which was so vividly expressed by Sassoon and Owen, we are all too painfully aware of inflated rhetoric, grandiloquent generalities and a strain of sentimentality exemplified in the last six lines of 'The Dead':

Blow, bugles, blow! They brought us, for our dearth,
Holiness, lacked so long, and Love, and Pain.
Honour has come back, as a king, to earth,
And paid his subjects with a royal wage;
And Nobleness walks in our ways again;
And we have come into our heritage.

The most telling criticism of these sonnets came from a fellow-soldier and fellow-poet, Charles Hamilton Sorley, several years younger than Brooke, who was also killed in 1915. He wrote in a letter to his mother, after seeing Brooke's death announced in the *Morning Post*:

That last sonnet sequence of his which you sent me the review of in the *Times Lit. Supp.* and which has been so

praised, I find (with the exception of that beginning
'These hearts were woven of human joys and cares,
washed marvellously with sorrow' which is not about
himself) over-praised. He is far too obsessed with his own
sacrifice, regarding the going to war of himself (and
others) as a highly intense, remarkable and sacrificial
exploit, whereas it is merely the conduct demanded of him
(and others) by the turn of circumstances, where non-
compliance with this demand would have made life
intolerable. It was not that 'they' gave up anything of that
list he gives in one sonnet; but that the essence of these
things had been endangered by circumstances over which
he had no control, and he must fight to recapture them.
He has clothed his attitudes in fine words: but he has
taken the sentimental attitude.

At the same time, to his brother Ken he wrote: 'All
illusions about the splendour of war will, I hope, be gone
after the war.'

Brooke was a highly sensitive and intelligent young
man; and it is difficult to conceive that, if he had not been
killed by sun-stroke and blood-poisoning, and had survived the Gallipoli massacre to fight in the war of attrition
on the Western Front, he would not have written poetry so
far removed from that of Sassoon and Owen. The last
poem we have of his, 'Fragment', written on the troopship
that was taking him to the Aegean, shows a changing
mood, a firmer grasp, escaping former rhetoric, of the true
human implications of the war:

> I strayed about the deck, an hour, to-night
> Under a cloudy moonless sky; and peeped
> In at the windows, watched my friends at table,
> Or playing cards, or standing in the doorway,
> Or coming out into the darkness. Still
> No one could see me.
>   I would have thought of them
> – Heedless, within a week of battle – in pity,

Pride in their strength and in the weight and firmness
And link'd beauty of bodies, and pity that
This gay machine of splendour'ld soon be broken,
Thought little of, pashed, scattered. . . .
                    Only, always,
I could but see them – against the lamplight – pass
Like coloured shadows, thinner than filmy glass,
Slight bubbles, fainter than the wave's faint light,
That broke to phosphorous out in the night,
Perishing things and strange ghosts – soon to die
To other ghosts – this one, or that, or I.

Charles Sorley himself had only one volume of poems published, *Marlborough and Other Poems*, and that posthumously, in 1916. Only twenty years old when he died in the Battle of Loos, he nevertheless gives the impression of a mind already more mature than Brooke's, and a poetic gift, in spite of its youthful imperfections, that might have developed to far more impressive achievements than he had already shown. His letters, a selection of which was also published posthumously, realistic, well balanced, shrewd and ironical in judgment, increase the sense of loss to English letters that his early death must arouse. Of Scottish ancestry, he came from an academic family settled in Cambridge, passed his schooldays at Marlborough College, which he seems to have enjoyed, being intelligent and good at games, and instead of going up to Oxford at once when he had gained a scholarship in December 1913, spent six months in Germany. He conceived a deep, almost loving admiration for the country; though increasingly aware of the darker side of German culture, the militaristic spirit and the anti-Semitism, he applauded the efficiency, the love of learning and music and the simple patriotism that pervaded the country, 'the most enterprising nation in the world'. And yet, when the war broke out, he appears to have been quite clear that the

Allied cause was just, and that it was his business as an
Englishman to fight for his country for all the faults that he
saw in it. He returned home on 6 August 1914, and
applied for a commission at once. He could nevertheless
write to a friend on 10 August: 'I could wager that out of
twelve million eventual combatants there aren't twelve
who really want it.' His cherished hope was expressed in
his sonnet 'To Germany':

> You are blind like us. Your hurt no man designed,
> And no man claimed the conquest of your land.
> But gropers both through fields of thought confined
> We stumble and we do not understand.
> You only saw your future bigly planned,
> And we, the tapering paths of our own mind,
> And in each other's dearest ways we stand,
> And hiss and hate. And the blind fight the blind.
>
> When it is peace, then we may view again
> With new-won eyes each other's truer form
> And wonder. Grown more loving-kind and warm
> We'll grasp firm hands and laugh at the old pain,
> When it is peace. But until peace, the storm
> The darkness and the thunder and the rain.

The realistic, totally unsentimental cast of his mind is
shown in another sonnet, 'When You See Millions of the
Mouthless Dead', which must have been one of the last
that he wrote, a far cry from Brooke:

When you see millions of the mouthless dead
Across your dreams in pale battalions go,
Say not soft things as other men have said,
That you'll remember. For you need not so.
Give them not praise. For, deaf, how should they know
It is not curses heaped on each gashed head?
Nor tears. Their blind eyes see not your tears flow.
Nor honour. It is easy to be dead.
Say only this, 'They are dead.' Then add thereto,

'Yet many a better one has died before.'
Then, scanning all the o'ercrowded mass, should you
Perceive one face that you loved heretofore,
It is a spook. None wears the face you knew.
Great death has made all his for evermore.

Perhaps the most remarkable of his poems is the one
sometimes called 'Route March', which must be one of the
most bitter-tasting marching songs ever written, with its
insistence on the apartness of the earth from men's
suffering and death, and yet its oneness with them in their
fate. The ironic counterpointing of the lilting rhythm to
represent the heedless singing of the soldiers beside the
fact that they are singing on the way to probable anni-
hilation, is something, I believe, never before attempted:

> All the hills and vales along
> Earth is bursting into song,
> And the singers are the chaps
> Who are going to die perhaps.
> > O sing, marching men,
> > Till the valleys ring again.
> > Give your gladness to earth's keeping,
> > So be glad, when you are sleeping.
>
> Cast away regret and rue,
> Think what you are marching to.
> Little live, great pass.
> Jesus Christ and Barabbas
> Were found the same day.
> This died, that went his way.
> > So sing with joyful breath.
> > For why, you are going to death.
> > Teeming earth will surely store
> > All the gladness that you pour.
>
> Earth that never doubts nor fears,
> Earth that knows of death, not tears,

Earth that bore with joyful ease
Hemlock for Socrates,
Earth that blossomed and was glad
'Neath the cross that Christ had,
Shall rejoice and blossom too
When the bullet reaches you.
   Wherefore, men marching
   On the road to death, sing!
   Pour your gladness on earth's head,
   So be merry, so be dead.

From the hills and valleys earth
Shouts back the sound of mirth,
Tramp of feet and lilt of song
Ringing all the road along.
All the music of their going,
Ringing swinging glad song-throwing,
Earth will echo still, when foot
Lies numb and voice mute.
   On, marching men, on
   To the gates of death with song.
   Sow your gladness for earth's reaping,
   So you may be glad, though sleeping.
   Strew your gladness on earth's bed,
   So be merry, so be dead.

Another poet who belongs to the 'Rupert Brooke' period
of the war, an early volunteer like Sorley (he was born two
years earlier than Sorley, in 1893), but who was invalided
out after a brief period of service with the Royal Artillery,
was Robert Nichols. His second collection of war poems,
Ardours and Endurances, had a considerable vogue when it
was published in 1917, but he is little read nowadays, and
is seen as a rather bombastic and self-regarding purveyor
of the kind of semi-heroic rhetoric about war experience
that was to die a final death after Sassoon's 'Counter-
Attack'. In his prose work, *Goodbye to all That* (published in
1929), Graves writes of Nichols in disparaging tones:

Another poet on Boar's Hill was Robert Nichols, one more neurasthenic ex-soldier, with his flame-opal ring, his wide-brimmed hat, his flapping arms, and a 'mournful grandeur in repose' (the phrase comes from a review by Sir Edmund Gosse). Nichols served only three weeks in France, with the gunners, and got involved in no show; but, being highly strung, he got invalided out of the army and went to lecture on British war-poets in America for the Ministry of Information. He read Siegfried's poetry and mine, and started a legend of Siegfried, himself and me as the new Three Musketeers, though the three of us had never once been together in the same room.

It must at the same time be admitted that Nichols became one of his own most severe critics. In the Introduction to his volume of selected poems (1915–1940), he writes of his war poetry:

In my own case – that of an exceedingly guileless, highly emotional and inordinately romantic youth, steeped in the *Chanson de Roland* and Vigny's *Servitudes et Grandeurs Militaires* – my feelings were characterised by a vehemence and unity such as I have but rarely experienced since. I accordingly reject the majority of the poems in which I tried to express those feelings not because I am ashamed of having been possessed by those feelings, but because I now see my expression of them to have been callow and crude.

Characteristic of this vehemence, in Whitman-esque mood, with genuine feeling warring against the rhetoric, but with no hint of the disillusionment that was to underline poems on similar themes later in the war, is his poem 'Casualty':

> They are bringing him down,
> He looks at me wanly.
> The bandages are brown,

Brown with mud, red only –
But how deep a red! in the breast of the shirt,
Deepening red too, as each whistling breath
Is drawn with the suck of a slow-filling squirt
While waxen cheeks waste to the pallor of death.
O my comrade!
My comrade that you could rest
Your tired body on mine, that your head might be laid
Fallen and heavy – upon this my breast,
That I might take your hands in my hands
To chafe! That abandoned your body might sink
Upon mine, which here helplessly, grievously stands;
That your body might drink
Warmth from my body, strength from my veins,
Life from my heart that monstrously beats,
Beats, beats and strains
After you vainly!
The trench curves. They are gone.
The steep rain teems down.
O my companion!
Who were you? How did you come,
Looking so wanly upon me? I know –
And O, how immensely long I have known –
Those aching eyes, numb face, gradual gloom,
That depth without groan!
Take now my love – this love which alone
I can give you – and shed without pain –
That life if I could I would succour,
Even as it were
This, this, my poor own!

Just as Rupert Brooke's *1914 Sonnets* were read and re-read in the majority of homes, when at least one member of each family was serving in the British army on the Western Front, as a prophylactic against despair and the pain of imminent or actual loss, so another short poem, with little or no poetic value, was almost equally and symbolically popular, John McCrae's 'In Flanders Fields':

In Flanders fields the poppies blow
Between the crosses, row on row
  That mark our place; and in the sky
  The larks, still bravely singing, fly
Scarce heard amid the guns below.

We are the Dead. Short days ago
We lived, felt dawn, saw sunset glow,
  Loved and were loved, and now we lie
    In Flanders fields.

Take up our quarrel with the foe:
To you from failing hands we throw
  The torch; be yours to hold it high.
  If ye break faith with us who die
We shall not sleep, though poppies grow
    In Flanders fields.

MILITARY SERVICE ACT
1916

EVERY UNMARRIED MAN
of
MILITARY AGE

Not excepted or exempted under this Act
CAN CHOOSE
ONE OF TWO COURSES:

(1) He can **ENLIST AT ONCE** and join the Colours without delay;

(2) He can **ATTEST AT ONCE UNDER THE GROUP SYSTEM** and be called up in due course with his Group.

If he does neither, a third course awaits him:
HE WILL BE DEEMED TO HAVE ENLISTED
under the Military Service Act
ON THURSDAY, MARCH 2nd, 1916.

**HE WILL BE PLACED IN THE RESERVE.
AND BE CALLED UP IN HIS CLASS.**
as the Military Authorities may determine.

Voluntary enlistment was abandoned in favour of conscription by the
Military Service Act, 27 January 1916

3

Owen and Sassoon

BY 1916 the war of attrition on the Western Front had begun in deadly earnest. The high hopes of an early decisive victory, on one side or the other, had all died. The High Commands, both Allied and German, were nevertheless obsessed with the idea that an enormously increased weight of bombardment, and a far greater readiness to throw ever huger armies into the battle, would turn the scales. This horrible idea, in which fighting men were treated simply as numbers to be expended, had its almost inevitable result. The old, superbly trained German army had almost vanished already in the holocaust; the British Expeditionary Force and the finest cadres of the French army had been replaced by conscripted levies who, like the new German soldiers, could not match the inspiration and traditional pride of the ancient regiments. The discredited idea of reckless frontal attack still held its deathly grip on the minds of the generals, on the Allied side especially in view of the possibilities of the new weapon they had introduced, the armoured fighting vehicle, or tank.

The result was the Battle – or Battles – of the Somme, which followed the enormously costly French defence of their fortress of Verdun. After many months of attack and counter-attack, the battle died down, with grotesquely little change in the entrenched positions on either side of

the hostile lines in France and Flanders. The British lost
60,000 men in the first day's fighting round the Somme;
their total loss in the battle has been reckoned at 410,000
men (dead and seriously wounded), the French losses at
190,000 and the German losses at nearly half a million.

This carnage, and stalemate, could not fail to have its
effect on the minds of the intelligent and articulate soldiers
in the field. The last tattered rags of the Rupert Brooke
mood were blown away. The two most outstanding poets
of the new mood were Sassoon and Owen.

Siegfried Sassoon, born in 1886, a year before Brooke,
came from a well-to-do family, on his father's side
descended from the merchant bankers who made their
fame and fortune in the East. He was educated at Marlborough and Cambridge, without distinguishing himself
scholastically at either school or university; but in his
earliest years developed a passion for outdoor games and
sports. In his first autobiographical book (*Memoirs of a
Fox-Hunting Man*) he describes how cricket, golf, horse-
riding and hunting came to absorb more and more of his
time and his dreams. He joined up as a trooper in the
Yeomanry two days before war broke out, and soon after
was given a commission in the 'Special Reserve' and sent
out to France. He began writing poetry early – in fact as a
boy – but his first poems written during his wartime
service show little more than his deeply ingrained love of
the countryside, his belief in England's cause and the
sense of 'fighting for our freedom'.

It was only later, as his experience of actual fighting
deepened, that his highly sensitive nature began to feel
that the truth about soldiers' life in the trenches and what
he saw of death and suffering around him must be
recorded. He was evidently a fearless soldier, and though
he has stated that in his regiment he was only known as
'Kangaroo' and never, as Graves maintained, as 'Mad
Jack', there is no doubt that he was capable of brave and

even reckless exploits against the enemy on his own
initiative. But his personal bravery did not interfere with
his growing conviction that too deep a psychological gulf
existed between the Home Front, the civilians of England,
and the army and what it went through in France. He felt
that it was time that illusions were dispelled in England,
that everyone should know of the continuing horror and
tragedy of the war of attrition, and reckon for themselves
whether the slaughter and the agony were worth the, to
him, rapidly evaporating ideals with which the war had
been started. The Battle of the Somme deepened this
mood, and he began to write poems, bitter, satirical and,
as he has said himself, 'deliberately written to disturb
complacency'. It is nevertheless a fact that they have
lasted far longer than would have been the fate of mere
'poster-art' in poetry: the feeling is too deep and too
sincere, the expression too masterly. Many of them were
written while on sick leave in England, from notes he had
made during the fighting. There are, to begin with, purely
satirical short pieces, such as 'They', in which he attacked
the attitude of the Anglican church at home:

The Bishop tells us: 'When the boys come back
They will not be the same; for they'll have fought
In a just cause: they lead the last attack
On Anti-Christ; their comrades' blood has bought
New right to breed an honourable race,
They have challenged Death and dared him face
                               to face.'

'We're none of us the same!' the boys reply.
'For George lost both his legs; and Bill's stone blind;
Poor Jim's shot through the lungs and like to die;
And Bert's gone syphilitic: you'll not find
A chap who's served that hasn't found *some* change.'
And the Bishop said: 'The ways of God are strange!'

The eight lines of 'Blighters' are even more savage:

The House is crammed: tier beyond tier they grin
And cackle at the Show, while prancing ranks
Of harlots shrill the chorus, drunk with din;
'We're sure the Kaiser loves our dear old Tanks!'

I'd like to see a Tank come down the stalls,
Lurching to rag-time tunes, or 'Home, sweet Home,' –
And there'd be no more jokes in music-halls
To mock the riddled corpses round Bapaume.

Sometimes a note of deep sadness appears to modify the
bitterness, as in 'Does it Matter?':

Does it matter? – losing your legs? . . .
For people will always be kind,
And you need not show that you mind
When the others come in after hunting
To gobble their muffins and eggs.

Does it matter? – losing your sight? . . .
There's such splendid work for the blind;
And people will always be kind,
As you sit on the terrace remembering
And turning your face to the light.

Do they matter? – those dreams from the pit? . . .
You can drink and forget and be glad,
And people won't say that you're mad;
For they'll know that you've fought for your country,
And no one will worry a bit.

More rarely Sassoon attempted a longer, more realistic
descriptive piece, which achieves its effect by the mount-
ing horror of its details of action, as in the poem which
gave its name to his second volume of war poems,
'Counter-Attack':

11 Propaganda poster of 1918: tanks did have a decisive influence on the
war that year, although until then their use had been rather ineffective

12 Siegfried Sassoon, in 1915

13 Wilfred Owen, *c.* 1914

Through Darkness
to Light
**THE ONLY ROAD
FOR AN ENGLISHMAN**
Through Fighting
to Triumph

14 This poster reflected the conviction in the High Command from 1916
onwards that the only way to victory was to throw more and more men into
battle. The attitude resulted in long-drawn-out battles, such as the Battle of
the Somme in which 600,000 allies died

15, 16 Battles continued to drag on fruitlessly during 1917: *above*, British troops crossing the Somme in March; *below*, the Battle of Passchendaele, aptly named by Lloyd George 'the battle of the mud', was perhaps the most savage and futile of the war

17 C. R. W. Nevinson, *La Mitrailleuse*, 1915

18, 19 Trenches and barbed wire on the Western Front created conditions of siege where army manoeuvre was impossible

20, 21 Over 700,000 British soldiers had died by 1918: *above*, wounded soldiers at a dressing station in 1917; *below*, a dead soldier in the Battle of Tardenois, July 1918

We'd gained our first objective hours before
While dawn broke like a face with blinking eyes,
Pallid, unshaved and thirsty, blind with smoke.
Things seemed all right at first. We held their line,
With bombers posted, Lewis guns well placed,
And clink of shovels deepening the shallow-trench.
The place was rotten with dead; green clumsy legs
High-booted, sprawled and grovelled along the saps;
And trunks, face downward in the sucking mud,
Wallowed like trodden sand-bags loosely filled;
And naked sodden buttocks, mats of hair,
Bulged, clotted heads, slept in the plastering slime.
And then the rain began, – the jolly old rain!

A yawning soldier knelt against the bank,
Staring across the morning blear with fog;
He wondered when the Allemands would get busy;
And then, of course, they started with five-nines
Traversing, sure as fate, and never a dud.
Mute in the clamour of shells he watched them burst
Spouting dark earth and wire with gusts from hell,
While posturing giants dissolved in drifts of smoke.
He crouched and flinched, dizzy with galloping fear,
Sick for escape, – loathing the strangled horror
And butchered, frantic gestures of the dead.

An officer came blundering down the trench:
'Stand-to and man the fire-step!' On he went . . .
Gasping and bawling, 'Fire-step . . . counter-attack!'

Then the haze lifted. Bombing on the right
Down the old sap: machine-guns on the left;
And stumbling figures looming out in front.
'O Christ, they're coming at us!' Bullets spat,
And he remembered his rifle . . . rapid fire . . .
And started blazing wildly . . . then a bang
Crumpled and spun him sideways, knocked him out
To grunt and wriggle: none heeded him; he choked
And fought the flapping veils of smothering gloom,
Lost in a blurred confusion of yells and groans . . .

Down, and down, and down, he sank and drowned,
Bleeding to death. The counter-attack had failed.

When, after a further period on the Western Front, he
was posted to the Near East, some of his poems revealed
that his mind was still running on the scenes he had
witnessed in France; for instance, a poem most deeply
tinged with the homo-erotic feeling that runs through his
work, 'I Stood with the Dead':

I stood with the Dead, so forsaken and still:
    When dawn was grey I stood with the Dead.
And my slow heart said, 'You must kill, you must kill:
    Soldier, soldier, morning is red.'

On the shapes of the slain in their crumpled disgrace
    I stared for a while through the thin cold rain . . .
'O lad that I loved, there is rain on your face,
    And your eyes are blurred and sick like the plain.'

I stood with the Dead . . . They were dead; they were
                                                    dead;
    My heart and my head beat a march of dismay:
And gusts of the wind came dulled by the guns . . .
    'Fall in!' I shouted; 'Fall in for your pay!'

It is a curious fact that when Sassoon came to write
Memoirs of an Infantry Officer in 1930 (under the disguise
name of Sherston for his central character), several of the
episodes which form the stark subjects of his poems of the
time suffer a modification, or rather mollification of effect.
Here, for instance, is 'Lamentations', written in 1917:

I found him in a guard-room at the Base.
From the blind darkness I had heard his crying
And blundered in. With puzzled, patient face
A sergeant watched him; it was no good trying
To stop it; for he howled and beat his chest.

And, all because his brother had gone west,
Raved at the bleeding war; his rampant grief
Moaned, shouted, sobbed, and choked while he was
                                                kneeling
Half-naked on the floor. In my belief
Such men have lost all patriotic feeling.

In Sassoon's prose description of the same episode seventeen years later, the terse, ironic conclusion has been replaced by a comment in a very different key:

After groping. about in the dark and tripping over tent ropes I was beginning to lose my temper when I opened a door and found myself in a Guard Room. A man, naked to the waist, was kneeling in the middle of the floor, clutching at his chest and weeping uncontrollably. The Guard were standing around with embarrassed looks, and the Sergeant was beside him, patient and unpitying. While he was leading me to the blanket store I asked him what was wrong. 'Why, sir, the man's been under detention for assaulting the military police, and now 'e's just 'ad news of his brother being killed. Seems to take it to heart more than most would. 'Arf crazy, 'e's been, tearing his clothes off and cursing the War and the Fritzes. Almost like a shell-shock case, 'e seems. It's his third time out. A Blighty one don't last a man long nowadays, sir.' As I went off into the gloom I could still hear the uncouth howlings.
    'Well, well; this is a damned depressing spot to arrive at!' I thought, while I lay awake trying to keep warm and munching a bit of chocolate, in a narrow segment of a canvas shed about four feet high.

In 1917, after his first book of war poems, *The Old Huntsman*, had been published, Sassoon's revulsion against a war that he felt could be honourably brought to an end by an armistice between the Allies and the Germans, both sides realizing that they had nothing to

gain by the prolongation of a fruitless, extravagantly
costly and increasingly demoralizing slaughter, led him
to the point of total rejection, a belief that he could no
longer square it with his conscience to go on fighting in
such a war. In this crisis, while convalescing after a spell
in hospital, he prepared a statement for his commanding
officer, which ran as follows:

I am making this statement as an act of wilful defiance of
military authority, because I believe that the War is being
deliberately prolonged by those who have the power to
end it. I am a soldier, convinced that I am acting on behalf
of soldiers. I believe that this War, on which I entered as a
war of defence and liberation, has now become a war of
aggression and conquest. I believe that the purpose for
which I and my fellow soldiers entered upon this war
should have been so clearly stated as to have made it
impossible to change them, and that, had this been done,
the objects which actuated us would now be attainable by
negotiation. I have seen and endured the sufferings of the
troops, and I can no longer be a party to prolong these
sufferings for ends which I believe to be evil and unjust. I
am not protesting against the conduct of the war, but
against the political errors and insincerities for which the
fighting men are being sacrificed. On behalf of those who
are suffering now I make this protest against the deception
which is being practised on them; also I believe that I may
help to destroy the callous complacency with which the
majority of those at home regard the contrivance of
agonies which they do not, and which they have not
sufficient imagination to realize.

Sassoon made his brave gesture of defiance and revolt
in the summer of 1917. Largely owing to the personal
persuasions and intervention behind the scenes of his
fellow-soldier and fellow-poet Robert Graves (who
appears in *Memoirs of an Infantry Officer* as David
Cromlech), he was not court-martialled, as he had

TELEGRAMS : "WARHOSPITAL, SLATEFORD."
TELEPHONE : CENTRAL 2850.

"Dottyville."

CRAIGLOCKHART WAR HOSPITAL,

SLATEFORD,

MIDLOTHIAN.

July. 26 -

My dear Robbie.

There are 160 officers here, most of them half-dotty. No doubt I'll be able to get some splendid details for future use . .

Rivers - the chap who looks after me, is very nice - I am very glad to have the chance of talking to such a fine man.

Do you know anyone amusing in Edinburgh who I can go & see?

It was very jolly seeing Robert G. up here. we had great fun on his birthday - ate enormously. R. has done some very good poems which he repeated to me. He was supposed to escort me up here; but missed the train & arrived 4 hours after I did!

Hope you aren't worried about my social position. yrs ever. S

(327)

A letter written by Siegfried Sassoon to friend and poet Robert Ross
from Craiglockhart military hospital, July 1917. In it he refers to Robert
Graves

originally expected, but eventually sent as a shell-shock case to Craiglockhart military hospital near Edinburgh, where he was under the care of a brilliant and sympathetic neurologist, Dr W. H. R. Rivers. It was there, a few weeks later, that an event occurred that was to be of the greatest import to the future of English poetry.

Among his fellow patients was Owen, some seven years younger, who already knew Sassoon by repute, and was a fervent admirer of his poetry. One day he appeared in Sassoon's room with several copies of *The Old Huntsman* under his arm, which he asked Sassoon to autograph for himself and some of his friends. He then admitted that he wrote poems himself, and shyly asked Sassoon to look at them. Sassoon was impressed by them and they became close friends; on Owen's side this friendship developed into a hero-worship that was almost love. Under Sassoon's influence and gentle but pertinent criticism, Owen began that series of poems which has made his fame: an 'annus mirabilis', such as his beloved Keats had once experienced, between that summer of 1917 and his death in action just before the end of the war.

Wilfred Owen was born in March 1893 in Oswestry in Shropshire. The family moved from there to Shrewsbury, then to Birkenhead and then back to Shrewsbury, where Owen entered Shrewsbury Technical School as a day boy until 1911 when he matriculated at London University (but only with a pass). Instead of pursuing a university career, he took a job as pupil and lay reader to a Rev. Herbert Wigan, but was not happy there, and in the summer of 1913 decided to go to France. He began as a teacher of English at the Berlitz School in Bordeaux, but in July 1914 took the opportunity to become tutor to two boys in a Catholic family also in Bordeaux, during which time he met and made friends with the French poet Laurent Tailhade, who gave him intelligent encouragement in the poetry he was already beginning to write.

While he was staying in Bordeaux he visited the war hospital there and witnessed operations performed without anaesthetic on the early wounded of the war. Finally he returned to England in the late summer of 1915, and very soon after joined the Artists' Rifles, was commissioned in the Manchester Regiment in June 1916, and sailed for France in December of the same year, attached to the Lancashire Fusiliers. He was wounded on three occasions in 1917 and, sensitive and highly strung by temperament, with his nerves in poor shape, was sent to the Welch Hospital in Netley in mid-June 1917. About a week later he was transferred to Craiglockhart. He was pronounced fit enough to be sent back to the fighting line in the late summer of 1918, was awarded an M.C. for outstanding bravery in October, but in November, only a week before the Armistice, was killed trying to get his men across the Sambre canal.

Like Sassoon, Owen appears to have thought of his poems as manifestos, truthful reports on what was happening at the Front far deeper in their revelation than anything the war correspondents could or would write. While Sassoon wanted in many of his poems to shock the complacent public in England to the realities of war, to the inefficiency of its higher direction and the ghastly suffering behind the cold communiqués, Owen wanted to stir compassion at its deepest levels for what was going on every day in the war areas, to make the public ask itself what end the unceasing casualties – on both sides – were serving. In the introduction for the volume of poems he envisaged (never published in his lifetime), he wrote:

Above all I am not concerned with poetry. My subject is war, and the pity of war. The Poetry is in the pity. Yet these elegies are to this generation in no sense consolatory. They may be to the next. All the poet can do is to warn. That is why true poets must be truthful.

The truth is, of course, that if he had not become a poet of increasingly technical assurance and originality, capable of an astonishing musical orchestration in his finest and most mature poems, the compassion that he intended to be the major emotion aroused in his poetry would not have had the profound effect on the minds of his contemporaries – and of subsequent generations – that has undoubtedly taken place. Sassoon's shorter pieces, with their irony, compression and intensity, fine and memorable as they are, are more nearly poster-poems compared with the best of Owen's; I doubt if Owen could have written them, for his gifts did not lie that way. But Sassoon's longer descriptive poems, such as 'Counter-Attack', where he attempted more complex and tragic effects, fail to achieve the haunting resonance of Owen's more purely elegiac poems, such as 'Exposure'. 'Counter-Attack' magnificently carries out Sassoon's basic intention of revealing and shocking, but it does not reach the deeper levels of imaginative power that Owen alone of the war poets was to make his own.

Owen's most famous and most anthologized poem, 'Strange Meeting', seems likely to have been inspired, whether consciously or unconsciously, by the fifth canto of Shelley's *Revolt of Islam* (*Laos and Cythna*):

> And one whose spear had pierced me, leaned beside,
>   With quivering lips and humid eyes; – and all
> Seemed like some brothers on a journey wide
>   Gone forth, whom now strange meeting did befall
>   In a strange land, round one whom they might
>   call
> Their friend, their chief, their father, for assay
>   Of peril, which had saved them from the thrall
> Of death, now suffering. Thus the vast array
> Of those fraternal bonds were reconciled that day.

Owen's poem confines itself to the meeting after death,
or in dreams, of one English soldier and a German soldier
he had killed:

It seemed that out of battle I escaped
Down some profound dull tunnel, long since scooped
Through granites which titanic wars had groined.
Yet also there encumbered sleepers groaned,
Too fast in thought or death to be bestirred.
Then, as I probed them, one sprang up, and stared
With piteous recognition in fixed eyes,
Lifting distressful hands as if to bless.
And by his smile, I knew that sullen hall,
By his dead smile I knew we stood in Hell.
With a thousand pains that vision's face was grained;
Yet no blood reached there from the upper ground,
And no guns thumped, or down the flues made moan.
'Strange friend,' I said, 'here is no cause to mourn.'
'None,' said the other, 'save the undone years,
The hopelessness. Whatever hope is yours,
Was my life also; I went hunting wild
After the wildest beauty in the world,
Which lies not calm in eyes, or braided hair,
But mocks the steady running of the hour,
And if it grieves, grieves richlier than here.
For of my glee might many men have laughed,
And of my weeping something had been left,
Which must die now. I mean the truth untold,
The pity of war, the pity war distilled.
Now men will go content with what we spoiled,
Or, discontent, boil bloody, and be spilled.
They will be swift with swiftness of the tigress.
None will break ranks, though nations trek from
                                                   progress.
Courage was mine, and I had mystery,
Wisdom was mine, and I had mastery:
To miss the march of this retreating world
Into vain citadels that are not walled.

Then, when much blood had clogged their
                                                    chariot-wheels,
I would go up and wash them from sweet wells,
Even with truths that lie too deep for taint.
I would have poured my spirit without stint
But not through wounds; not on the cess of war.
Foreheads of men have bled where no wounds were.
I am the enemy you killed, my friend.
I knew you in this dark: for so you frowned
Yesterday through me as you jabbed and killed.
I parried; but my hands were loath and cold.
Let us sleep now. . . .'

This mysterious, harrowing and prophetic poem is remarkable technically for its use of assonance, or pararhyme, to increase the effect of half-reality, half-dream that pervades it. Owen used assonance in a number of other poems, but nowhere more tellingly, it seems to me, than in 'Strange Meeting'. In his fine article on Owen in *Noble Essences*, Sir Osbert Sitwell suggests that Owen thought of the trick of varying the vowel sounds in a rhyme while keeping the consonants the same, as something that he had discovered for himself. It is, however, a fact that, for instance, Henry Vaughan, Emily Dickinson and G. M. Hopkins had all used it in one poem or another. It is equally true that there is no proof that Owen had read any of these three poets, and it is certain that Hopkins at least cannot have been known to him.

Some of Owen's best-known poems were written as bitterly ironic comments on, near parodies of, well-known Romantic poems. An outstanding instance of this is the way he turned Swinburne's 'Before the Mirror' inside out in 'Greater Love'. Swinburne's first two stanzas run:

> White rose in red rose-garden
>   Is not so white;
> Snowdrops that plead for pardon

And pine for fright
  Because the hard East blows
Over their maiden rows
    Grow not as this face grows from pale to bright.

Behind the veil, forbidden
    Shut up from sight,
Love, is there sorrow hidden,
    Is there delight?
  Is joy thy dower or grief,
White rose of weary leaf,
    Late rose whose life is brief, whose loves are light?

It is easy to imagine Owen's feeling of scorn and
revulsion against this languidly exotic mood when he sat
down to write 'Greater Love':

Red lips are not so red
  As the stained stones kissed by the English dead.
Kindness of wooed and wooer
Seems shame to their love pure.
O Love, your eyes lose lure
  When I behold eyes blinded in my stead!

Your slender attitude
  Trembles not exquisite like limbs knife-skewed,
Rolling and rolling there
Where God seems not to care;
Till the fierce love they bear
  Cramps them in death's extreme decrepitude.

Your voice sings not so soft, –
  Though even as wind murmuring through raftered
                                                    loft, –
Your dear voice is not dear,
Gentle, and evening clear,
As theirs whom none now hear,
  Now earth has stopped their piteous mouths that
                                                    coughed.

Heart, you were never hot
  Nor large, nor full like hearts made great with shot;
And though your hand be pale,
Paler are all which trail
Your cross through flame and hail:
  Weep, you may weep, for you may touch them not.

As his convictions about the war as he witnessed it grew
with his technical assurance, Owen was in no mood to
qualify his determination to tell the truth – his truth – and
to make the most sharp-edged poetry possible out of his
vision. When Graves suggested to him that he should
sometimes write more cheerful poems, Owen's answer
was to send him one of his greatest poems, in which his
irony, his uncompromising realism and his compas-
sionate fellow-feeling with the sufferings of the soldiers he
led and amongst whom he lived in the midst of the fighting
are expressed as a counterpoint to and transposition of the
'merriment' that Graves appeared to be looking for. He
called it 'Apologia Pro Poemate Meo':

I, too, saw God through mud, –
  The mud that cracked on cheeks when wretches
                                       smiled.
  War brought more glory to their eyes than blood,
  And gave their laughs more glee than shakes a child.

Merry it was to laugh there –
  Where death becomes absurd and life absurder.
  For power was on us as we slashed bones bare
  Not to feel sickness or remorse of murder.

I, too, have dropped off fear –
  Behind the barrage, dead as my platoon,
  And sailed my spirit surging light and clear
  Past the entanglement where hopes lay strewn;

And witnessed exultation –
  Faces that used to curse me, scowl for scowl,

Shine and lift up with passion of oblation,
Seraphic for an hour; though they were foul.

I have made fellowships –
Untold of happy lovers in old song.
For love is not the binding of fair lips
With the soft silk of eyes that look and long,

By Joy, whose ribbon slips, –
But wound with war's hard wire whose stakes are
        strong;
Bound with the bandage of the arm that drips;
Knit in the webbing of the rifle-thong.

I have perceived much beauty
In the hoarse oaths that kept our courage straight;
Heard music in the silentness of duty;
Found peace where shell-storms spouted reddest
        spate.

Nevertheless, except you share
With them in hell the sorrowful dark of hell,
Whose world is but the trembling of a flare,
And heaven but as the highway for a shell,

You shall not hear their mirth:
You shall not come to think them well content
By any jest of mine. These men are worth
Your tears. You are not worth their merriment.

Sassoon himself, in *Siegfried's Journey*, wrote with per-
ceptive generosity of Owen's poetry:

His manuscripts show that he seldom brought his poems
to their final form without considerable re-casting and
revision. There was a slowness and sobriety in his method,
which was, I think, nondramatic and elegiac rather than
leapingly lyrical. I do not doubt that, had he lived longer,
he would have produced poems of sustained grandeur

and ample design. It can be observed that his work is prevalently deliberate in movement. Stately and processional, it has the rhythm of emotional depth and directness and the verbal resonance of one who felt in glowing primary colours and wrote with solemn melodies in his mind. . . . His mouth was resolute and humorous, his eyes long and heavy-lidded, quiescent rather than penetrating. They were somewhat sleepy eyes, kind, shrewd, and seldom lit up from within. They seemed, like much else in his personality, to be instinctively guarding the secret sources of his inward power and integrity.

In one of his letters to a friend Owen wrote a revealing passage about his development as a poet. In hospital, just after his return from France, he had been reading a biography of Tennyson which maintained that Tennyson was never a happy person, in spite of all his success and honours and the comforts of his life:

I can quite believe he never knew happiness for one moment such as I have – for one or two moments. But as for misery was he ever frozen alive with dead men for comforters? Did he ever hear the moaning at the bar, not at twilight and evening bell only, but at dawn, noon and night, eating and sleeping, watching and waking, always the close moaning of the Bar; the thunder, the hissing and the whining of the Bar? – Tennyson, it seems, was always a great child. So should I have been but for Beaumont Hamel.

4

Graves and Blunden

IN *Goodbye To All That*, thinking of the mood of 1917, Robert Graves writes that, 'Osbert and Sacheverell Sitwell, Herbert Read, Siegfried, Wilfred Owen and myself, and most other young writers of the time, none ... believed in the war'. Although an understatement of the revulsion that these poets had come to feel against the war by 1917, these words do sum up the total change of mood in the work of all of them in the second phase of the war.

Graves was born in 1895 in Wimbledon into a middle-class family of strong literary and musical interests. His grandfather, who was of ancient Irish descent, became Protestant Bishop of Limerick, and married a Scots-woman of equally ancient family. On his mother's side he was descended from the famous German historian, Leopold von Ranke. There were thus many racial strands in his ancestry, a combination that has so often produced children of exceptional character and gifts. Graves went to six different preparatory schools, and eventually to the public school of Charterhouse, where he began writing poetry, and conceived a crush on a younger boy which haunted him throughout the war, though as an adult he became heterosexual. War was declared just after he had finished his schooling, and he enlisted at once in the Royal Welch Fusiliers.

He published two volumes of poetry, *Over the Brazier* in 1916, and *Fairies and Fusiliers* in 1917. But the surprising thing about Graves as a war poet is that, in his *Collected Poems* (1914–47), he eliminated all poems that had any reference to war, except one, 'Recalling War', which was written twenty years later. These *Collected Poems*, many of which are extremely remarkable, forceful and original in language and approach, give the impression that underneath the often sinister fantasies, the fragmented episodes of legend and myth, some horror-laden experience was being deeply suppressed and struggling to break through the grotesque shapes and goblins, the esoteric symbols that dominate them. The war is there, as it were, but only in indirect paraphrase and mime. They are extremely disturbing to the imagination.

Whatever Graves himself may have decided in later years, there are a number of poems he wrote during the war years that do not deserve to be forgotten. One short poem, 'The Last Post', written in June 1916, is particularly moving and impressive:

> The bugler sent a call of high romance –
> 'Lights out! Lights out!' to the deserted square:
> On the thin brazen notes he threw a prayer,
> 'God, if it's *this* for me next time in France . . .
> O spare the phantom bugle as I lie
> Dead in the gas and smoke and roar of guns,
> Dead in a row with the other broken ones,

Lying so stiff and still under the sky
Jolly young Fusiliers, too good to die.'
The music ceased, and the red sunset flare
Was blood about his head as he stood there.

Another striking poem, with an ironic twist at the end
which is in a vein that recalls, though without imitation,
some of Sassoon's more acerbic productions of the time, is
'The Leveller':

Near Martinpuich that night of hell
Two men were struck by the same shell,
Together tumbling in one heap
Senseless and limp like slaughtered sheep.

One was a pale eighteen-year-old,
Blue-eyed and thin and not too bold,
Pressed for the war not ten years too soon,
The shame and pity of his platoon.

The other came from far-off lands
With bristling chin and whiskered hands,
He had known death and hell before
In Mexico and Ecuador.

Yet in his death this cut-throat wild
Groaned 'Mother! Mother!' like a child,
While that poor innocent in man's clothes
Died cursing God with brutal oaths.

Old Sergeant Smith, kindest of men,
Wrote out two copies there and then
Of his accustomed funeral speech
To cheer the womenfolk of each: –

'He died a hero's death: and we
His comrades of "A" Company
Deeply regret his death: we shall
All deeply miss so true a pal'.

The poem written so many years later, 'Recalling War', has that mixture of nostalgic realism, vivid and original imagery and the sardonic eye that characterizes the mature Graves:

Entrance and exit wounds are silvered clean,
The track aches only when the rain reminds.
The one-legged man forgets his leg of wood,
The one-armed man his jointed wooden arm.
The blinded man sees with his ears and hands
As much or more than once with both his eyes.
Their war was fought these twenty years ago
And now assumes the nature-look of time,
As when the morning traveller turns and views
His wild night-stumbling carved into a hill.

What, then, was war? No mere discord of flags
But an infection of the common sky
That sagged ominously upon the earth
Even when the season was the airiest May.
Down pressed the sky, and we, oppressed, thrust out
Boastful tongue, clenched fist and valiant yard.
Natural infirmities were out of mode,
For Death was young again: patron alone
Of healthy dying, premature fate-spasm.

Fear made fine bed-fellows. Sick with delight
At life's discovered transitoriness,
Our youth became all-flesh and waived the mind.
Never was such antiqueness of romance,
Such tasty honey oozing from the heart.
And old importances came swimming back –
Wine, meat, log-fires, a roof over the head,
A weapon at the thigh, surgeons at call.
Even there was a use again for God –
A word of rage in lack of meat, wine, fire,
In ache of wounds beyond all surgeoning.

War was return of earth to ugly earth,
War was foundering of sublimities,

Extinction of each happy art and faith
By which the world had still kept head in air,
Protesting logic or protesting love,
Until the unendurable moment struck –
The inward scream, the duty to run mad.

And we recall the merry ways of guns –
Nibbling the walls of factory and church
Like a child, piecrust; felling groves of trees
Like a child, dandelions with a switch.
Machine-guns rattle toy-like from a hill,
Down in a row the brave tin-soldiers fall:
A sight to be recalled in elder days
When learnedly the future we devote
To yet more boastful visions of despair.

One finds it difficult to imagine that Owen, if he had
survived the war (as he so nearly did), could have written
such a poem with its almost jaunty note of detachment
and (never sentimentalizing) acceptance.

It seems more than likely that Graves will be remembered in the annals of literature for his autobiographical
prose work, *Goodbye To All That*, first published at the
moment when the serious public began to be ready to
think again about, to relive the war, in 1929, and re-
published (and much improved) in 1957. It is a full autobiography, from his childhood to the breakup of his
marriage and his departure from England to live in
Majorca in 1929; but by far the longer part of it is devoted
to his war service. Among one's strongest impressions
when reading that part of it is that he cared almost
obsessively about the traditions and good name of his
regiment, as if belonging to the Royal Welch Fusiliers
satisfied some deep unconscious impulse in him to be a
regular soldier. It is written with extraordinary vividness:
the scenes of battle are gripping and yet, though never
unfeeling and never shirking the details of horrible death

and mutilation, such grisly details are never over-emphasized with retrospective emotionalism. The description of the Battle of Loos, with its endless confusion, unnecessary slaughter and waste, acts of heroism and sudden collapse of nerve in some of the soldiers, is a magnificent piece of descriptive dramatic writing. What is more, his narrative is enlivened throughout by pictures of eccentric and colourful characters and incidents; it is full of humorous and sometimes painful anecdotes. These are always telling because of the cool tone of a sensitive civilian turned tough and courageous soldier who had resolved that the 'only way out of the war is the way through it', which is kept up with economical mastery. He shared Sassoon's growing disgust with the pointless human waste of the war and his sense of growing alienation from the ignorant and illusion-drugged 'people at home', but he believed that Sassoon was wrong in the pacifist protest to which his desperation finally drove him. *Goodbye To All That* is only by implication a condemnation of the murderous futility into which the First World War sank, but no less effective for that.

He describes his first encounter with Sassoon, with its surprising circumstances:

A day after I arrived [at the quarters of the First Battalion of his regiment] I went to visit 'C' Company men, where I got a friendly welcome. I noticed *The Essays of Lionel Johnson* lying on the table. It was the first book I had seen in France (except my own Keats and Blake) that was neither a military textbook nor a rubbishy novel. I stole a look at the flyleaf, and the name was Siegfried Sassoon. Then I looked around to see who could possibly be called Siegfried Sassoon and bring Lionel Johnson with him to the First Battalion. The answer being obvious, I got into conversation with him, and a few minutes later we set out for Bethume, being off duty until dusk, and talked about poetry.

In spite of his later doubts about Sassoon's 'protest', Graves realized and admired his nonchalant and idiosyncratic fearlessness. He describes a later episode:

The battalion's next objective was 'The Quadrangle', a small copse this side of Mametz Wood, where Siegfried distinguished himself by taking, single-handed, a battalion frontage which the Royal Irish Regiment had failed to take the day before. He went over with bombs in daylight, under covering fire from a couple of rifles, and scared away the occupants. A pointless feat, since instead of signalling for reinforcements, he sat down in the German Trench and began reading a book of poems he had brought with him. When he finally went back he did not even report. Colonel Stockwell, then in command, raged at him – the attack on Mametz Wood had been delayed for two hours because British patrols were still reported to be out. 'British Patrols' were Siegfried and his book of poems.

One of the most bizarre stories Graves relates is how, during the Battle of the Somme, he was officially posted as 'died of wounds' while still alive, though he had been severely wounded:

I was semi-conscious now and aware of my lung-wound through a shortness of breath. It amused me to watch the little bubbles of blood, like scarlet soap-bubbles, which my breath made in escaping through the opening of the wound.

It so happened, he tells us, that one of his aunts, who was in France to visit a South Wales Borderer nephew, discovered him in the same Rouen hospital and at once wrote to reassure his mother. Graves treats the whole episode as a great joke, and was tickled by the letters of condolence which, his mother informed him, she had eventually received. He wrote to Sassoon: 'By the way, I died on my 21st birthday. I can never grow up now.'

When one or the other was on leave or in hospital in England, Graves and Sassoon wrote each other affectionate letters, often long and intimate. One of the most interesting things that Graves records is his discovery of Sorley, and how Sorley's poems grew on him 'more and more'. While in hospital in Harlech he also discovered John Skelton, who was to become a great favourite of his. During his convalescence he visited Garsington, the famous wartime home of Philip Morrell and his wife Lady Ottoline, where he found the Sitwells, Robert Ross and Nichols, and was evidently fascinated by his hostess: 'Lady Utterly Immoral is such a ripper.' At the end of October 1917 he sent Sassoon a long letter, trying to reason him out of his anti-war stand: his chief arguments were that they had made a contract to be soldiers in the war, and contracts must be kept; and that by refusing to fight any longer, Sassoon would be alienating the sympathy of the very people he wanted to influence – 'the Bobbys and Tommys'. These arguments failed to sway Sassoon in his new, long-considered resolution; but Graves, though in part-sympathy with his views about the changed nature of the war, showed the strength of his feeling for Sassoon, as I have already related, by pulling every string he could behind the scenes to prevent him being court-martialled (which would quite clearly have embarrassed the War Office in the case of a distinguished and well-known officer who had won the M.C.), and getting him to accept a final medical examination, which pronounced him to be suffering from profound shell-shock and in need of psychiatric treatment: a turn of events which, so luckily for English poetry, brought him together with Owen at Craiglockhart.

The strong bonds of friendship between Sassoon and Graves do not, however, seem to have fully survived the publication of *Goodbye To All That*. In a copy of the first edition of the book, also rather caustically annotated in the margin by Blunden (and now in the New York Public Library, Berg Collection), Sassoon continually complains of Graves's confused inaccuracy, exaggeration and distortion of the facts. In particular he was shocked by Graves's statement that, because Owen had been accused of cowardice by his commanding officers (an allegation which has been strongly disputed, and attributed by Sassoon to C. K. Scott-Moncrieff), he was in a 'very shaky condition'. In his revised edition of the book Graves completely removed this remark.

Another poet who, like Graves, is more likely to be remembered for his reminiscences was Edmund Blunden, a countryman born and bred and a lover of Clare and the country tradition in English poetry. He wrote a number of poems, still deeply moving and characteristic of the man and his attitude to the war; and yet more powerful is his summing up of his war experiences in his prose work, *Undertones of War* (1928). I do not rate it quite as highly as

that masterpiece, *Goodbye To All That* (in its revised
edition), but I nevertheless find it a moving and
memorable book. By comparison with Graves its tone is
quiet and ruminative, and in contrast Graves sometimes
seems almost too cockily self-assured, even at times
histrionic: Graves and Blunden were very different
characters. In the last sentence of *Undertones of War*
Blunden describes himself as 'a harmless young shepherd
in a soldier's coat'. That is, perhaps, too self-deprecating,
but what is striking and entirely individual about
Blunden's work is the sense that obsessed him all through
his war service of the deeply loved countryside in contrast
to the ruined landscape that bombs and shells had made
of the Flanders scene; one even feels that it was that strong
belief in the beauty of nature and its inevitable recovery
from the gruesome way the war was punishing and
despoiling it that kept him sane among the horrors he was
experiencing.

It has been objected by some (to me insentient) critics
that his continual reference to the gentle charms of
unspoilt countryside marks him as an unrepentant
Georgian; but one writes out of love for what one is deeply
attached to and what evokes the deepest layers of one's
imaginative world, and there is nothing half-hearted,
shallow or sentimental about Blunden's spiritual
identification with meadows, trees, flowers and the wild
creatures that roam among them, one might say the
countryside as nature intended; in fact it seems to me to
give unique strength to his work. He is a master of the
telling, small incident, as in this description of a dog he
found in the midst of battle:

It was Geoffrey Salter speaking out firmly in the darkness.
Stuff Trench – this was Stuff Trench; three feet deep,
corpses under foot, corpses on the parapet. . . . Moving
along as he spoke with quick emotion and a new power

22 An advance dressing station on the Montauban-Guillemont road, September 1916

23 A group of officers with Edmund Blunden bottom right, *c.* 1917

24 Edward Thomas with his son Mervyn, in 1900

26 Ivor Gurney, in 1915

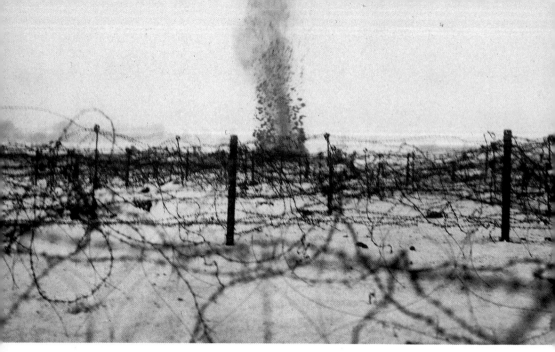

27 Shell bursting amongst barbed wire on the battlefield of Beaumont
Hamel, December 1916

28 The remains of the Menin Road, near Gheluvelt, September 1916

29 Paul Nash, *Wire*, 1918–19

30 Paul Nash, *The Ypres Salient at Night*, 1918

31 C. R. W. Nevinson, *The Harvest of Battle*, 1919

32 Adrian Hill, *Road Menders*, c. 1917

(for hitherto his force of character had not appeared in the less exacting sort of war), he began to order the newcomers into sentry-groups; and stooping down to find what it was snuffing at my boots I found it was a dog. He was seemingly trying to keep me from treading on a body. I caught sight of him by someone's torch or flare; he was black and white; and I spoke to him, and at the end of a few moments he allowed me to carry him off. Cassells and myself had finished, and returned by ourselves by the shortest way; now the strain told, our feet weighed like lead, and our hope was out of action. I put down the dog, who came limpingly round the shadowy shell-holes, stopped, whined, came on again; what was the use? he perhaps thought; that way, too, there is this maniacal sport of high explosives, and the mud is evidently the same all over the wood; I shall stay here. Warmly I wished to adopt this dog, but now I could scarcely stoop, and I reflected that the mud and shell zone extended a long way on; so there he stayed; feebly I passed along.

Early on in his book he describes how strange it was, when he first came to the Front, to pass through a landscape recovering from the state of total ruin in which it had been – and was soon to be again – which made it in itself a memorial to an already almost distant war:

History and nature were beginning to harmonize in the quiet of that sector. In the orchard through which we passed immediately, wagons had been dragged together once with carts and farm gear to form barricades; I felt that they should never be disturbed again, and the memorial raised near there to the dead of 1915 implied a closed chapter. The empty farm houses were not yet effigies of agony or mounds to punished, atomized material; they could still shelter, and they did. Their hearths could still boil the pot. Acres of self-sown wheat glistened and sighed as we wound our way between, where rough scattered pits recorded a hurried firing-line of long ago. Life, still abundant sang here and smiled; the

lizard ran war-less in the warm dust; and the ditches were
trembling quick with odd tiny fists, in worlds as remote
as Saturn.

Even in the full fury of fighting and horror that disgusts
the senses, Blunden is aware of nature still surviving,
however tenuously, around him:

Who had been there for but a few hours could ever forget
the strange spirit and mad lineaments of Cuinchy? A
mining sector, as this was, never lost the sense of hovering
horror. That day I arrived in it the shimmering aching
heat blurred the scene, but a trouble was at once
discernible, if indescribable, also rising from the ground.
Over Coldstream Lane, the chief communication trench,
deep red poppies, blue and white corn flowers and darnel
thronged the way to destruction; the yellow cabbage-
flowers thickened here and there in sickening brilliance.
Giant thistles made a thicket beyond. There the ground
became torn and vile, the poisonous breath of such
explosions skulked all about, and the mud which choked
the narrow passages stank as one pulled through it, and
through the twisted, disused wires running mysteriously
onward. Much lime was wanted at Cuinchy, and that had
its ill savour, and often its horrible meaning.

One touching scene is recorded – touching because so
at variance with what inevitably followed – of ordinary
craftsmen going about their work in the intervals of battle:

My trench maintenance parties with hammers and
choppers, saws and nails were lodged in Hamel village;
they made themselves comfortable in cellars, and went to
and fro in the exact and ordinary manner of the British
working man. One, by turns, stayed at home to cook; the
others kept the line tidy, and left no staircase, recess nor
buttress unbeautified. They enjoyed this form of active
service with pathetic delight – and what men were they?
Willing, shy, mostly rather like invalids, thinking of their
families. Barbusse would have 'got them wrong', save in

this: they were all doomed. Almost all finished their peaceful lives a few days afterwards in the fury at Stuff Trench.

The records of the First World War show that almost as great a peril and source of misery as that of shells and bombs seems to have been that of rain, rain that caused the squelching mud of the trenches and the almost impassable bog of no-man's-land when an attack was ordered, a bog in which only slightly wounded men might disappear for ever. Blunden records unforgettably such a moment of, not man-made, but natural disaster:

And then the Brigade headquarters came, beautiful to look upon, and their red tabs glowed out of several shell-holes. This was more than the German observers could endure, and in a short time there was such a storm of high explosives on that small space that the brains of the Brigade withdrew, a trifle disillusioned, to the old British trenches. Another storm, and a more serious and incontestable one, was now creeping on miserably with grey vapours of rain over the whole field. It was one of the many that caused the legend, not altogether dismissed even by junior officers, that the Germans could make it rain when they wanted to . . . I went out to visit company headquarters, which were now (with bombs and note-books) under waterproof sheets stretched over shell holes, swiftly becoming swimming baths. As the unprepossessing evening came, N. C. Olive and myself were sharing a tin of 'Sunshine' sausages in one of these pools.

Nature, surviving and reviving nature, spoke always to Blunden in his war years, at the worst of the crises, but he tells us frankly that he derived comfort and calm also from books of poetry he had brought with him, books of a sort that it seems unlikely any other British soldier had chosen to bring with him. Sassoon and Graves had their Lionel Johnson and their Sorley, but Blunden writes that for him:

During this period my indebtedness to an eighteenth-
century poet became enormous. At every spare moment I
read in Young's *Night Thoughts of Life, Death and
Immortality*, and I felt the benefit of this grave and
intellectual voice, speaking out of a profound eighteenth-
century calm, often in metaphors which came home to one
even in a pill-box. The mere amusement of discovering
lines applicable to our crisis kept me from despair.

Blunden's best poems of this period, many of which are
collected in the concluding pages of *Undertones of War*, are
full of the same sentiments, the same moods rendered with
quiet poetic assurance; as in this stanza from 'At Senlis
Once':

O how comely it was and how reviving
When with clay and with death no longer striving
Down firm roads we came to houses
With women chattering and green grass thriving.

With a grimmer irony he wrote, in 1917, 'Rural
Economy':

There was winter in those woods
    And still it was July:
There were Thule solitudes
    With thousands huddling nigh;
There the fox had left his den,
The scraped holes hid not stoats but men.

To these woods the rumour teemed
    Of peace five miles away;
In sight, hills hovered, houses gleamed
    Where last perhaps we lay
Till the cockerels bawled bright morning and
The hours of life slipped the slack hand.

In sight, life's farms sent forth their gear,
    Here rakes and ploughs lay still,

Yet, save some curious clods, all here
    Was raked and ploughed with a will.
The sower was the ploughman too,
And iron seeds broadcast he threw.

What husbandry could outdo this?
    With flesh and blood he fed
The planted iron that nought amiss
    Grew thick and swift and red,
And in a night though ne'er so cold
Those acres bristled a hundredfold.

Why, even the wood as well as field
    This thoughtful farmer knew
Could be reduced to plough and tilled
    And if he planned, he'd do;
The field and wood, all bone-fed loam,
Shot up a roaring harvest home.

Perhaps the most impressive, the most comprehensive of all Blunden's war poetry, is his long blank-verse poem, 'Third Ypres', both deeply characteristic and more tragic in its implications than many of his shorter poems, a summing-up of the worst of his war experience. Particularly effective are the following lines:

                  The grey rain,
Steady as the sand in an hourglass on this day,
Where through the window the red lilac looks,
And all's so still, the chair's odd click is noise –
The rain is all heaven's answer, and with hearts
Past reckoning we are carried into night
And even sleep is nodding here and there.
The second night steals through the shrouding rain.
We in our numb thought crouching long have lost
The mockery triumph, and in every runner
Have urged the mind's eye see the triumph to come,
The sweet relief, the straggling out of hell
Into whatever burrows may be given

For life's recall. Then the fierce destiny speaks.
This was the calm, we shall look back for this.
The hour is come; come, move to the relief!
Dizzy we pass the mule-strewn track where once
The ploughman whistled as he loosed his team;
And where he turned home-hungry on the road,
The leaning pollard marks us hungrier turning.
We crawl to save the remnant who have torn
Back from the tentacled wire, those whom no shell
Has charred into black carcasses – Relief!
They grate their teeth until we take their room,
And through the churn of moonless night and mud
And flaming burst and sour gas we are huddled
Into the ditches where they bawl sense awake,
And in a frenzy that none could reason calm,
(Whimpering some, and calling on the dead)
They turn away: as in a dream they find
Strength in their feet to bear back that strange whim
Their body.

5

Gurney, Harvey and Thomas

ANOTHER soldier poet who was deeply rooted in
his rural homeland, and was conscious (as the title
of his first book of poems *Severn and Somme* indicates) all
through his war service of the contrast between the
peaceful country scenes of the Severn valley and the stark,
war-torn landscape of Flanders, was Ivor Gurney. He
found his greatest happiness as a boy in wandering about
the meadows, the hills, copses and wild pathways round
his home. The range of his poetic achievement is not
perhaps as wide or effective as Blunden's, nor as skilful
and varied rhythmically, but he left at least a dozen poems
that are deeply moving and individual, before he slipped
gradually into madness – a paranoid schizophrenia
accentuated but by no means entirely brought on by war
experience – which led to him being confined in an asylum
between 1922 and his death in 1937. His sensibility was

acute, but it seems probable that music was as much, perhaps more, his true mode of expression as poetry. His songs in particular have been highly praised for their delicate originality of mood and characteristically English harmonies; four volumes of them had been published by 1957, as well as song cycles composed to accompany the poems of A. E. Housman and Edward Thomas; but it still seems too early to form a just assessment of them in relation to his poetry.

Gurney was born in 1890, in Gloucester, and was therefore six years older than Blunden. His family was professional, lower middle-class, but his unusual qualities soon came to the notice of his teachers, and especially of the Rev. Alfred Cheeseman, who found gifted young male adolescents especially attractive and had a notable capacity for bringing out their talents. He learned to play the violin; while his sister Emily learned the piano. At the age of twenty-one he was awarded a scholarship at the Royal College of Music. It was worth £40; but the devoted Cheeseman managed to get it doubled. At the outbreak of war he felt strongly that he should enlist, but was rejected at first on the grounds of defective eyesight; at his second attempt, in 1915, he was accepted and enlisted in the 2nd/5th Gloucesters. He was sent to France in May 1916, and was therefore a serving soldier in the Battle of the Somme. He was gassed in 1917, and that was the end of his war service; he took a long time to recover, and before his recovery was complete his mental instability had reasserted itself.

Two older women friends played an important part in his life and affections. The first, Margaret Hunt, who was fifteen years his senior, had almost certainly been introduced to him by Cheeseman; while the second, Marion Scott, also unmarried, and thirteen years older than him, became his friend and patron while he was at the Royal College. Some of his most informative and moving letters while he was at the Front were written to these two friends. The way his thoughts kept returning to his beloved Gloucestershire countryside is poignantly shown by a letter to Marion Scott in May 1917:

O for a garden to dig in, and music and books in a house of one's own, set in a little valley from whose ridges one may see the Malverns and the Welsh Hills, the plain of Severn and the Severn Sea; to know oneself free there from the drill-sergeant and the pack, and to order one's life years ahead – plans, doubtless to be broken, but sweet secure plans taking no account of fear or even Prudence but only Joy. One could grow whole and happy there, the mind would lose its sickness and grow strong; it is not possible that health should wait long from such steady and gently beautiful ways of life. The winter's hardships should steel one, the spring bring Joy, summer should perfect this Joy, and autumn bring increase and mellowness to all things, and set the seal of age and ease on things not before secure. I grow happy writing of it.

Professor Fussell has remarked on the peculiarly 'literary' element of the war in the minds of the English soldiers. Gurney did not see his experience as part of any continuity recorded in British poetry and history, as some of his fellow soldiers did, but his mind was full of the poetry he loved so much and could discuss with others of his generation whenever the war allowed an interval for such thoughts and deeper recorded memories. Sometime in 1916, in a letter to Catherine, the wife of the poet Lascelles Abercrombie, close friend of Brooke and one of the contributors to the first volume of *Georgian Poetry*, he wrote that he spent an evening out of the continuing nightmare, with Cymric comparison of a battalion to which his own battalion had been attached for instructions:

They are Welsh, mostly, and personally I feared a rather rough type. But, oh the joy, I crawled into a dugout, not high but fairly large, lit by a candle, and so met four of the most delightful young men that could be met anywhere. Thin faced and bright eyed, their faces showed beautifully against the soft glow of the candlelight, and their musical voices delightful after the long march at attention in silence. There was no sleep for me that night. I made up next day a little, but what then? We talked of Welsh folk song, of George Borrow, of Burns, of the RCM; of – yes – of Oscar Wilde, Omar Khayyam, Shakespeare, and of the war: distant from us by 300 yards. Snipers were continually firing, and rockets – fairy lights they call them, fired from a pistol – lit up the night outside. Every now and again a distant rumble of guns to remind us of the reason we were foregathered. They spoke of their friends dead or maimed in the bombardment, a bad one, of the night before, and in the face of their grief I sat there and for once self-forgetful, more or less, gave them all my love; for their tenderness, their steadfastness and kindness to raw fighters and *very* raw signallers.

The strong homo-erotic undertones in the poetry of these articulate British soldiers, evident in the quotations I have made from the poetry of Sassoon, Owen and Nichols, appear equally clearly in Gurney's 'To His Love', a poem that has an almost unbearably painful conclusion:

> He's gone, and all our plans
>   Are useless indeed.
> We'll walk no more on Cotswold
>   Where the sheep feed
>   Quietly and take no heed.
>
> His body that was so quick
>   Is not as you
> Knew it, on Severn river
>   Under the blue
>   Driving our small boat through.

You would not know him now . . .
  But still he died
Nobly, so cover him over
  With violets of pride
  Purple from Severn side.

Cover him, cover him soon!
  And with thick-set
Masses of memoried flowers –
  Hide that red wet
  Thing I must somehow forget.

One of Gurney's most original poems describes a scene of action in which he refuses a suggestion (clearly not an order) by an officer with 'a finicking accent' to advance through no-man's-land to certain death, and is upheld in the crisis by thoughts of music. Most of Sassoon's and Owen's poems report and expatiate on what they saw soldiers under their command suffer and experience. Here, in 'The Silent One', one of the cannon-fodder speaks for himself:

Who died on the wires, and hung there, one of two –
Who for his hours of life had chattered through
Infinite lovely chatter of Bucks accent:
Yet faced unbroken wires; stepped over, and went
A noble fool, faithful to his stripes – and ended.
But I weak, hungry, and willing only for the chance
Of line – to fight in the line, lay down under unbroken
Wires, and saw the flashes and kept unshaken,
Till the politest voice – a finicking accent, said:
'Do you think you might crawl through, there: there's
                                                    a hole.'
Darkness, shot at: I smiled, as politely replied –
'I'm afraid not, Sir.' There was no hole, no way to be
                                                    seen,
Nothing but chance of death, after tearing of clothes.
Kept flat, and watched the darkness, hearing bullets
                                                    whizzing –

And thoughts of music – and swore deep heart's deep
                                                    oaths
(Polite to God) and retreated and came on again,
Again retreated – and a second time faced the screen.

Before his mental collapse Gurney took to writing
poems in a kind of rhyming, jingling doggerel – but a
doggerel of genius – which is characteristic of almost all
the asylum poems. Here is one of the most vivid and
coherent, called 'The Bohemians':

Certain people would not clean their buttons,
Nor polish buckles after latest fashions,
Preferred their hair long, putties comfortable,
Barely escaping hanging, indeed hardly able,
In Bridge and smoking without army cautions
Spending hours that sped like evil for quickness,
(While others burnished brasses, earned promotions.)
These were those ones who jested in the trench,
While others argued of army ways, and wrenched
What little soul they had still further from shape,
And died off one by one, or became officers.
Without the first of dream, the ghost of notions
Of ever becoming soldiers, or smart and neat,
Surprised as ever to find the army capable
Of sounding 'Lights out' to break a game of Bridge,
As to fear candles would set a barn alight:
In Artois or Picardy they lie – free of useless fashions.

After he had been taken into a private asylum,
Barnwood, on the outskirts of Gloucester, Gurney never
recovered his mental equilibrium. He did not stay there
all the last years of his life and continued to write poetry
and compose music fitfully, but all the time he was subject
to delusions that he was being persecuted by telegraphic
messages which caused him much physical as well as
mental anguish. Some of the most poignant moments
during his incarceration were visits by Helen, widow of

Edward Thomas, whom he revered. On the second of
these visits she brought with her an ordnance map of the
surroundings of Gloucester. This was a brilliant inspiration, and it gave Gurney endless delight to trace and
visualize parts of the countryside, the lanes and fields
which he had known so well in his boyhood.

There exists a long tragic letter which he wrote, without
date but obviously near the end, which he addressed to the
London Metropolitan Police. These are the concluding
paragraphs:

The torments were bad; the courage deserving reward.
I have appealed to the Carnegie Trustees and the Royal
College to appeal for my death. My life was in many ways
so good – the best I ever led considering all things – when
so many times I stayed up all night to work or walk. . . .

The harm of such a life was small. Employment for but
approximately sixteen weeks only – because (roughly)
there was none to be had. I read the papers, occasionally
sought work, and strove as few can have striven perhaps to
work, or stay up.

An appeal is made for Justice, or Trial, or to be allowed
to die, or to receive Chance of Death. Many times daily
has the writer prayed for Death, and asks that his pain
may be ended, either by Death or Release. Having so
much use left in him, if he were free and allowed to get
well.

I should have been released after three weeks (by
instinct) or six weeks by assurance.

For six months and a half now my confinement and
pain has endured.

My music, my verses – my war service should have
saved me from so much pain.

So many times had I gone to honour, and really injured
none.

Asking for Death, Release or Imprisonment. An end to
pain.

A special place, among the lesser poets, belongs to F. W. Harvey who, like Gurney, was born in Gloucestershire, in 1888. He was taken prisoner in 1916, and spent the rest of the war in a prisoner-of-war camp. Many of the poems he wrote there, allowed through by the German censorship, were published in English periodicals. Though not in the first flight of poetry, they give unique expression to the frustrated emotions of those soldiers who were denied the experience of joining their countrymen in the fighting that continued; as for instance, 'Prisoners':

> Comrades of risk and rigour long ago
> Who have done battle under honour's name,
> Hoped (living or shot down) some need of fame,
> And wooed bright Danger for a thrilling kiss, –
> Laugh, oh laugh well, that we have come to this!
> Laugh, oh laugh loud, all ye who long ago
> Adventure found in gallant company!
> Safe in Stagnation, laugh, laugh bitterly,
> While on this filthiest backwater of Time's flow
> Drift we and rot, till something set us free!
>
> Laugh like old men with senses atrophied,
> Heeding no Present, to the Future dead,
> Nodding quite foolish by the warm fireside
> And seeing no flame, but only in the red
> And flickering embers, pictures of the past: –
> Life like a cinder fading black at last.

The passionate attachment to the English countryside and its sanative beauty in contrast to the ruined landscape of war, comes out clearly in the few poems which Edward Thomas wrote on themes connected with the fighting. He came late to the army – he enlisted in July 1915, already in his middle thirties, in the Artists' Rifles – as he came late to the writing of poetry. Desperately poor, and married early, he spent all the years of his early youth writing books about his wanderings on foot through southern

England, such as *The Icknield Way*, and biographies such as
his book on his beloved Richard Jeffries. Many were pot-
boilers, poorly rewarded, but it was impossible for him not
to go on writing them: bills were always piling up, needing
to be paid. He was, I think, increasingly aware of the vein
of poetry in him that was waiting to be exploited, and was
encouraged in his hope of becoming a poet by his
friendship with the American poet Robert Frost, who
spent some time in England from 1913 to 1915. Under
Frost's example, he began to write poetry in 1914; but
what fully released his poetic energies was, ironically
enough, the fact that when he joined up and then (in the
autumn of 1916) became an officer, his pay made it
possible for him to abandon all pot-boiling. From that
moment poetry began to pour out of him; and though his
fame was slow in coming, his reputation now stands high
among the poets of the first two decades of this century. It
will in my opinion stand higher still as the purity of his
musical language and deceptive simplicity of his style, his
mastery of his craft and absolute control of a manner that
is unmistakably his own, often deeply imbued with a
haunting melancholy and unmatched empathy with the
natural world, come to be appreciated in contrast with all
that is inflated, pretentious and self-consciously literary –
particularly in the English poetry that was being written
during his lifetime. Walter de la Mare, who knew him
well, wrote of him:

To be alone with him was a touchstone of everything
artificial and shallow, of everything sweet and natural in
the world in which we lived. One could learn and learn
from him not the mere knowledge of the living things and
scenes around us which were as familiar to him as his own
handwriting, but of their life in himself.

One will find nothing in Thomas's work of the bitter
protest against the squalor and horror of the war, but in

one poem which affirms his love of and belief in England,
'This is No Case of Petty Right or Wrong', he let himself
go about the profiteers and jingoists of the Home Front:

> This is no case of petty right or wrong
> That politicians or philosophers
> Can judge. I hate not Germans, nor grow hot
> With love of Englishmen, to please newspapers.
> Beside my hate for one fat patriot
> My hatred of the Kaiser is love true:–
> A kind of god he is, banging a gong.
> But I have not to choose between the two,
> Or between justice and injustice. Dinned
> With war and argument I read no more
> Than in the storm smoking along the wind
> Athwart the wood. Two witches' cauldrons roar.
> From one the weather shall rise clear and gay;
> Out of the other an England beautiful
> And like her mother that died yesterday.
> Little I know or care if, being dull,
> I shall miss something that historians
> Can rake out of the ashes when perchance
> The phoenix broods serene above their ken.
> But with the best and meanest Englishmen
> I am one in crying, God save England, lest
> We lose what never slaves and cattle blessed.
> The ages made her that made us from dust:
> She is all we know and live by, and we trust
> She is good and must endure, loving her so:
> And as we love ourselves we hate her foe.

More truly characteristic of his mood and way of
looking at the war before he went out to France is his poem
'As the Team's Head-Brass', a meditation and quietly
rendered country conversation with deeper undertones of
sorrow and loss at the partial breakdown of the natural
order of things, and yet also an implied optimism of a
surviving permanence. All this is conveyed without the

33 Sir William Orpen, *Dead Germans in a Trench*, *c.* 1919

34 Isaac Rosenberg, in 1917

35 Isaac Rosenberg. Self-portrait signed 'J.R. France July 1917'

36 Paul Nash, *Existence* (undated)

37 David Jones, scene in the trenches (undated)

38 David Jones, 'Huts, Winnal Down, Winchester, Oct. 26th 1915'

39 David Jones, soldier in a trench, 1916

40 David Jones, 'Huts, Winnal Down camp, Winchester, Oct. 26th 1915'

41 David Jones, 'Salisbury Plain, at musketing course, autumn 1915'

slightest suggestion of rhetoric or outraged emotion, and
yet says everything:

As the team's head-brass flashed out on the turn
The lovers disappeared into the wood.
I sat among the boughs of the fallen elm
That strewed the angle of the fallow, and
Watched the plough narrowing a yellow square
Of charlock. Every time the horses turned
Instead of treading me down, the ploughman leaned
Upon the handles to say or ask a word,
About the weather, next about the war.
Scraping the share he faced towards the wood,
And screwed along the furrow till the brass flashed
Once more.

        The blizzard felled the elm whose crest
I sat in, by a woodpecker's round hole,
The ploughman said. 'When will they take it away?'
'When the war's over.' So the talk began –
One minute and an interval of ten,
A minute more and the same interval.
'Have you been out?' 'No,' 'And don't want to,
                       perhaps?'
'If I could only come back again, I should.
I could spare an arm. I shouldn't want to lose
A leg. If I should lose my head, why, so,
I should want nothing more. . . . Have many gone
From here?' 'Yes.' 'Many lost?' 'Yes: a good few.
Only two teams work on the farm this year.
One of my mates is dead. The second day
In France they killed him. It was back in March,
The very night of the blizzard, too. Now if
He had stayed here we should have moved the tree.'
'And I should not have sat here. Everything
Would have been different. For it would have been
Another world.' 'Ay, and a better, though
If we could see all all might seem good.' Then
The lovers came out of the wood again.

The horse started and for the last time
I watched the clods crumble and topple over
After the ploughshare and the stumbling team.

Thomas was killed at Easter 1917: he had written less
than 150 poems, and none of them after he reached the
Front. He has a stature as a poet quite independent of the
circumstances of the war: if he had been involved at an
earlier stage of the fighting one can only conjecture how it
might have changed him; one cannot imagine that he
would have become an Owen or Sassoon, though perhaps
he was more in tune with Gurney. Even in his well-known
epitaph of an unnamed ploughman, 'A Private', killed
and, like thousands of others, unidentified in death, it is
the country scene of his homeland that so unemphatically
and yet so poignantly dominates the eight lines:

This ploughman dead in battle slept out of doors
Many a frozen night, and merrily
Answered staid drinkers, good bedmen, and all bores:
'At Mrs Greenland's Hawthorn Bush,' said he,
'I slept.' None knew which bush. Above the town,
Beyond 'The Drover', a hundred spot the down
In Wiltshire. And where now at last he sleeps
More sound in France – that, too, he secret keeps.

One might be tempted to say that the melancholy
which informs almost all the poems he wrote after 1914 –
which as far as one knows are *all* his poems – was an
indirect reflection of the war; and yet it is a melancholy
that can continually be heard in much of the prose he
wrote before the war broke out.

6

Read, Sitwell and Rosenberg

SIR Herbert Read, who was born in 1893 and was
therefore only twenty-one when the War broke out,
is – like Graves and Blunden – rather a special case because
the best of what he wrote about the War was produced
after its end. He served with especial distinction as a
captain in the Yorkshire Regiment and won the D.S.O. and
M.C. The two volumes of poems that were written
immediately out of his war experience, both published in
1919, *Naked Warriors* and *Ecologues*, Imagist in style and, as
he has observed himself, 'brutal and even ugly' in their
mood, have little that is memorable in them as Sassoon,
Owen and Gurney are memorable – that is, as poetry.
There is, however, a passage from one, 'My Company',

that voices outstandingly the exceptional feeling that grew
up between officers and their men under the stress of
companionship in action:

> And then our fights: we've fought together
> Compact, unanimous;
> And I have felt the pride of leadership.
>
> In many acts and quiet observances
> You absorbed me:
> Until one day I stood eminent
> And I saw you gather'd round me,
> Uplooking,
> And about you a radiance that seemed to beat
> With variant glow and to give
> Grace to our unity.
> But God! I know that I'll stand
> Someday in the loneliest wilderness,
> Someday my heart will cry
> For the soul that has been, but that now
> Is scatter'd with the winds,
> Deceased and devoid.
>
> I know that I'll wander with a cry:
> 'O beautiful men, O men I loved,
> O whither are you gone, my company?'

Curiously enough, Read did not see fit to publish until
1933 a long poem, *The End of a War*, which he had
written or started to write very soon after the Peace. It is
an extremely ambitious piece of work and full of moving
passages, and it has been much admired; yet, in my
judgment, it lacks as a whole the immediacy and sharp-
ness of imaginative vision – perhaps because of its
distance in time – that the extremely dramatic (and
horrible) incident around which it is written should have
called for. On the very day before the Armistice was
declared, the British were in pursuit of the retreating

Germans, who still doggedly harassed them with occasional interludes of machine-gun resistance. One British company encountered a seriously wounded German soldier, who told them that the village towards which they were advancing had already been evacuated. They moved on into the village and were ambushed by fire from all sides, many being killed. In their outraged shock at being so deceived they bayoneted all the Germans they could find, and then went back and killed the German officer who was the cause of the gruesome massacre. A little later the British soldiers discovered the savagely mutilated body of a young French girl covered with bayonet wounds. No one ever discovered what lay behind this atrocity; when the British soldiers assembled the next morning, the war was over.

Read divides his poem into three parts, or reflections: 'Meditation of a Dying German Officer', 'Dialogue between the Body and the Soul of the Murdered Girl', and 'Meditation of the Waking English Officer'. One of the most effective passages is where the German officer declares his faith, hopeless though he knows it has become, in the cause of his Fatherland. One cannot ignore the similarity between this and the concluding passage of Edward Thomas's 'This is no Case of Petty Right or Wrong':

Faith in self comes first, from self we build
the web of friendship, from friends to confederates
and so to the State. This web has a weft
in the land we live in, a town, a hill
all that the living eyes traverse. There are lights
given by the tongue we speak, the songs we sing,
the music and the magic of our Fatherland.
This is a tangible trust. To make it secure
against the tempest of inferior minds
to build it in our blood, to make our lives
a tribute to its beauty – there is no higher aim.

> This good achieved, then to God we turn
> for a crown on our perfection: God we create
> in the end of action, not in dreams.

Read's major contribution to the literature of the war produced by the combatants themselves is, however, his prose *In Retreat*. A short piece, of little more than 12,000 words, written in terse, economical sentences that maintain with the greatest skill a cool but vivid dramatic pace, it is as it were, a communiqué, but with a difference: Read not only gives the reader an exact account of his subject – the retreat of the British Fifth Army from St Quentin during the last big offensive of the Germans in March 1918 – but also of the human side, through innumerable small details that make it a major document of fighting action. There is no rhetoric or concealment of the conflicting emotions that possess the individuals who make up an army, under the extreme stress of one of the most intense experiences that modern war can produce. The highest praise that one can give it is that one feels that one was there. For instance:

Shortly after eleven o'clock, a gun team galloped madly down the main road. Then two stragglers belonging to the Machine-Gun Corps were brought to headquarters. They informed us that the front line had been penetrated. Later, an officer from the front-line battalion, with five or six men, came to us out of the mist. Most of the party were wounded, and as the officer's leg was being bandaged in the dugout, he told us his tale. He was haggard and incoherent, but the sequence was awfully clear to us. The enemy had attacked in great strength at 7.30. They had apparently reached the observation line unobserved, and overpowered the few men there before a warning could be given or an escape made. Advancing under cover of a creeping barrage, they had approached the main line of defence. No fire met them there, or only fire directed vaguely into the fog. The fight at the main line had been short and bloody. Our men, dazed and quivering after three hours' hellish bombardment (I could see them cowering on the cold mist-wet earth), had been brave to the limits of heroism; but pitifully powerless. The ghastly job had been completed by 8.30. About nine o'clock fresh enemy battalions passed through their fellows and advanced towards the front-line redoubt (L'Epine de Dallon). Our artillery fire must have been useless by then, still falling on the old enemy front line. At any rate, the enemy quickly surrounded the redoubt, and then penetrated it. This officer himself had been captured, and later had made his escape in the mist. He thought it possible that the headquarters of his battalion were still holding out.

We were still questioning our informant when an excited voice yelled down the dugout shaft: 'Boches on the top of the dugout.' Our hearts thumped. There was no reason why the enemy shouldn't be on us. They might have been anywhere in that damned mist. We drew our revolvers and rushed to the shaft. We did not mean to be caught like rats in a hole.

I remember my emotion distinctly: a quiet despair. I *knew* I went up those stairs either to be shot or bayoneted as I emerged, or, perhaps, to be made prisoner and so plunge into a strange unknown existence.

Half-way up the stairs, and a voice cried down: 'It's all right: they're our fellows.' Some artillerymen in overcoats, straggling across the open, had looked sinister in the mist.

We turned to the dugout, the released tension leaving us exhausted.

A moment of relaxation is described with the same skill and controlled narrative:

We went upstairs into an empty room. Two of us agreed to make a fire, while the other, the one who had given vent to his feelings, volunteered to go off in search of food. We split up wood we found in the house, and lit a fire. I took off my clothes to dry them, and sat on a bench in my shirt. If I had been asked then what I most desired, besides sleep, I think I would have said: French bread, butter, honey, and hot milky coffee.

The forager soon turned up. God only knows where he got that food from: we did not ask him. But it was French bread, butter, honey, and hot milky coffee in a champagne bottle! We cried out with wonder: we almost wept. We shared the precious stuff out, eating and drinking with inexpressible zest.

In Retreat is justly regarded as a masterpiece. Less effective, but often showing the same powers, are the six pieces that make up *Ambush* which followed, another pamphlet in the Criterion Miscellany, in 1930, of which 'Killed in Action' and 'The Raid' are outstanding. But Read had not done with the First World War. At a time when most of his fellow survivors had fallen silent, at the beginning of the Second World War, he wrote, what can be claimed, paradoxically, as his finest war poem of all, 'To a Conscript of 1940':

> *Qui n'a pas une fois désespère de l'honneur, ne sera jamais un héros.*   GEORGES BERNANOS

A soldier passed me in the freshly-fallen snow,
His footsteps muffled, his face unearthly grey;
And my heart gave a sudden leap
As I gazed on a ghost of five-and-twenty years ago.

I shouted Halt! and my voice had the old accustom'd
ring
And he obeyed it as it was obeyed
In the shrouded days when I too was one
Of an army of young men marching

Into the unknown. He turned towards me and I said:
'I am one of those who went before you

Five-and-twenty years ago: one of the many who never
returned,
Of the many who returned and yet were dead.

We went where you are going, into the rain and the
mud;
We fought as you will fight
With death and darkness and despair;
We gave what you will give – our brains and our blood.

We think we gave in vain. The world was not renewed.
There was hope in the homestead and anger in the
streets
But the old world was restored and we returned
To the dreary field and workshop and the immemorial
feud

Of rich and poor. Our victory was our defeat.
Power was retained where power had been misused
And youth was left to sweep away
The ashes that the fires had strewn beneath our feet.

But one thing we learned: there is no glory in the deed
Until the soldier wears a badge of tarnish'd braid;
There are heroes who have heard the rally and have
seen
The glitter of a garland round their head.

Theirs is the hollow victory. They are deceived.
But you, my brother and my ghost, if you can go
Knowing that there is no reward, no certain use
In all your sacrifice, then honour is reprieved.

To fight without hope is to fight with grace,
The self reconstructed, the false heart repaired.'
Then I turned with a smile, and he answered my salute
As we stood against the fretted hedge, which was like
white lace.

Osbert Sitwell will probably be remembered more for his prose than his poetry, and especially for his five-volume autobiography, *Left Hand, Right Hand*. He was born in December 1892, and was five years younger than his sister Edith and five years older than his brother Sacheverell, with both of whom he was associated in the public mind as an iconoclastic figure in the world of the arts. 'Goodbye you delightful but deleterious trio', Sir Edmund Gosse once remarked, according to Osbert. He joined the Grenadier Guards in 1912, and served throughout the war with his regiment. About his experiences he was extremely reticent in his autobiography, but he became more and more opposed to the continuance of the war as it dragged on from year to year and, as the casualties of his friends in the regiment steadily mounted, more embittered – and more despairing. He has left us only a small handful of poems that were inspired by those feelings, but has described to us how he suddenly felt inspired to write the poem 'Therefore the Name of it is called Babel' during his second period in the trenches, not far from Ypres. He sent it to his friend Richard Jennings, leader-writer and literary editor, who sent it to the editor of *The Times*, where it was published in May 1916:

> And still we stood and stared far down
> Into that ember-glowing town,
> Which every shaft and shock of fate
> Had shorn unto its base. Too late
>   Came carelessly Serenity.
>
> Now torn and broken houses gaze
> On to the rat-infested maze
> That once sent up rose-silver haze
>   To mingle through eternity.
>
> The outlines once so strongly wrought,
> Of city walls, are now a thought

Or jest unto the dead who fought . . .
   Foundation for futurity.

The shimmering sands where once there played
Children with painted pail and spade,
Are drearly desolate – afraid
   To meet night's dark humanity,

Whose silver cool remakes the dead,
And lays no blame on any head
For all the havoc, fire, and lead,
   That fell upon us suddenly,

When all we came to know as good
Gave way to Evil's fiery flood,
And monstrous myths of iron and blood
   Seem to obscure God's clarity.

Deep sunk in sin, this tragic star
Sinks deeper still, and wages war
Against itself; strewn all the seas
With victims of a world disease
– And we are left to drink the lees
Of Babel's direful prophecy.

This was, as Graves has already been quoted as
remarking, very closely in sympathy with the young
English poets who during the last two years of the war
were making their protest about what seemed to them the
total unwillingness of the politicians and generals to put
an honourable stop to the fruitless carnage. It was Robert
Ross who brought Sitwell and Owen together, in July
1918 when both were on leave and in London. Sitwell has
touchingly described an afternoon they spent together
under the mulberry trees in the Chelsea Physic Gardens,
only a few months before Owen was killed. A group of
Owen's most outstanding war poems was published in
Wheels, the annual magazine of contemporary poetry

which the Sitwells started towards the end of 1916, with Edith as editor, though she did not appear as such until 1918.

It is to Edith Sitwell's lasting credit that she spotted Owen as a magnificent poet at once. She was so deeply moved by what she had been shown for *Wheels* that she intended to issue a volume of all the poems under her editorship; but while she was preparing the volume she generously agreed to let his intimate friend and fellow-soldier, Sassoon, take over. When Isaac Rosenberg's *Poems* were published in 1922, she also immediately realized how outstanding he was, and wrote in her review in the *New Age* that 'Rosenberg was one of the two great poets killed in the war, the other being Wilfred Owen'. This was long before Dr F. R. Leavis announced his conversion and championship.

Rosenberg's high reputation now as a war poet and indeed as a poet of general promise who showed, especially in his verse drama *Moses*, that his war poetry was likely to have been only an episode in a long poetic career has, I cannot help feeling, rather obscured what he had already achieved and what he promised as a pictorial artist. Like Gurney, musician as well as poet, his power of artistic expression was twofold. Rosenberg's developing achievement as a draughtsman and painter has excited my admiration ever since I first saw the surviving work, even in reproduction. His later portraits have remarkable strength and a certain sculptured quality that some critics have also found in his poetry; while his best landscapes are firmly designed and have a power of conveying mood and atmosphere that are striking in so young an artist.

Unlike the poets with whom we have been dealing hitherto, Rosenberg came of a very poor background. His parents were émigré Russian (or rather Lithuanian) Jews of strong Orthodox faith who originally settled in Bristol, where Isaac was born in 1890, but seven years later left for the East End of London. His mother at first earned a living by embroidery while his father became a rather feckless pedlar. Rosenberg's original idea seems to have been to earn his living by his artistic aptitudes, but at the same time, from early on, he was determined to be a poet – and an English poet, not a Jewish poet. He read voraciously, particularly the Romantics, and it was some time before he discovered the poet who was to become his greatest admiration, John Donne. 1911 was an important year for him: he met three young Jewish intellectuals who were to become close and helpful friends: Joseph Leftwich (originally Lefkowitz), Simon Weinstein (who changed his name to Stephen Winsten) and John Rodker, who was later to become a publisher and translator of some reputation. In the same year he managed at last to be enrolled as a student in the Slade, mainly through the influence of Mrs Herbert Cohen, a well-to-do Jewish lady who became his part-patron and lent him money on a number of occasions.

The first encouragement of his poetry came in 1912 from the English poet Laurence Binyon, to whom he had sent a group of poems. Two years later he was introduced to Marsh's influential circle by the painter, Mark Gertler. Marsh, not uncharacteristically, found his poetry puzzling and obscure, but nevertheless saw promise in the drawings and paintings, encouraged him and purchased some.

His health had always been poor and, strongly advised by his doctors to try a change of climate, he managed to drum up funds for a trip to South Africa, with Marsh and others helping to find the fare. He left in the spring of 1914. While he was out there, war broke out. He returned in February 1915, and joined up a few months later.

His life in the army seems to have been a succession of humiliations and misfortunes. He was small, ugly by

conventional standards and scatter-brained about those
small points of discipline on which the army counts so
much. He was constantly getting into hot water, and
enduring punishments meted out by those who had no
glimmer of the fact that they were dealing with an
exceptional person rather than a confused and absent-
minded 'shirker', whose health in any case needed better
rations than he was getting.

There were, however, consolations for a man whose
dedication to his purpose of becoming poet and artist
never faltered. Lascelles Abercrombie, to whom some of
his poems had been shown in 1915, reacted warmly,
writing that he found a 'vivid and original impulse', and
that 'some of your phrases are remarkable; no one who
writes poetry could help envying some of them'. This
letter seems to have been a turning-point in Rosenberg's
self-confidence about his work. A small book containing
what he had written of *Moses* and a group of other shorter
poems was published in a small edition in a private
printing works. In the summer of 1916 this booklet was
shown to Robert Trevelyan, untiringly fluent poet and
close friend of the Bloomsbury Group, who wrote him a
letter full of admiration. This was followed by an even
more enthusiastic letter from Gordon Bottomley, another
contributor to the first volume of *Georgian Poetry*, a letter
which Rosenberg treasured to the end of his life, and
which made him feel that Marsh's continuing refusal to
find any exceptional merit in his poetry was ceasing to be
of prime importance. In understanding Marsh's attitude
one has to remember that after the deaths of Brooke and
Denis Browne he was a broken man. Rosenberg was
granted ten days' leave in September 1916. He returned to
active service in the winter of 1917–18, and was killed in
action in April 1918.

Now that we have all the poetry written by the com-
batant poets of the First World War before us – or all that

we seem in any case ever likely to have – what cannot fail to strike us about Rosenberg's contribution is that, though he hated the war, it is neither a poetry of protest, as Sassoon's was intended to be, nor of compassion to shock the non-combatants and higher direction of the war at home out of their insensitivity, as Owen's was, nor harrowingly to contrast the idyllic and natural life of the countryside into what war had done to it, as Blunden's and Gurney's was. He quite simply aimed to show the most terrible face of life as it was in his immediate experience and as it had always been in historic warfare. No poem of his shows this attitude of mind more clearly than his short 'Soldier: Twentieth Century':

> I love you, great new Titan!
> Am I not you?
> Napoleon and Caesar
> Out of you grew.
>
> Out of unthinkable torture,
> Eyes kissed by death,
> Won back to the world again,
> Lost and won in a breath,
>
> Cruel men are made immortal,
> Out of your pain born.
> They have stolen the sun's power
> With their feet on your shoulders worn.
>
> Let them shrink from your girth,
> That has outgrown the pallid days,
> When you slept like Circe's swine,
> Or a word in the brain's ways.

Nor, in a more complex and less rhetorical mood, in 'Returning, We Hear the Larks', does he shirk the paradoxical contrast between the still miraculous beauty of natural life as it managed somehow to survive in spite of guns and shells, and the dread in the hearts of human beings who know what they may have to face, indeed have already found, in this orgy of mutual destruction:

> Sombre the night is.
> And though we have our lives, we know
> What sinister threat lurks there.
>
> Dragging these anguished limbs, we only know
> This poison-blasted track opens on our camp –
> On a little safe sleep.
>
> But hark! joy – joy – strange joy.
> Lo! heights of night ringing with unseen larks.
> Music showering on our upturned list'ning faces.
>
> Death could drop from the dark
> As easily as song –
> But song only dropped,
> Like a blind man's dreams on the sand
> By dangerous tides,
> Like a girl's dark hair for she dreams no
>   ruin lies there,
> Or her kisses where a serpent hides.

A rejoicing lark in that poem; in another, 'Break of Day in the Trenches', there is a 'droll rat', the whole intention of which is to survive, ignorant of the calculating reasons of opposing armies and their discipline, its 'sardonic' attitude life's comment on two confronting lines of soldiers dedicated to killing one another at such close quarters that it can run from one to the other with impunity with its dangerous 'cosmopolitan sympathies'. Rosenberg concludes with a powerful double image of a poppy which he plucks from a parapet and the symbolic poppies 'whose roots are in man's veins' which he cannot thus save:

The darkness crumbles away –
It is the same old druid Time as ever.
Only a live thing leaps my hand –
A queer sardonic rat –
A I pull the parapet's poppy
To stick behind my ear.
Droll rat, they would shoot you if they knew
Your cosmopolitan sympathies.
Now you have touched this English hand
You will do the same to a German –
Soon, no doubt, if it be your pleasure
To cross the sleeping green between.
It seems you inwardly grin as you pass
Strong eyes, fine limbs, haughty athletes
Less chanced than you for life,
Bonds to the whims of murder,
Sprawled in the bowels of the earth,
The torn fields of France.
What do you see in our eyes
At the shrieking iron and flame
Hurled through still heavens?
What quaver – what heart aghast?
Poppies whose roots are in man's veins
Drop, and are ever dropping;
But mine in my ear is safe,
Just a little white with the dust.

It is generally agreed that the longer 'Dead Man's Dump' is his finest poem, in fact one of the finest poems to come out of the war. He describes, in the opening stanzas, the movement of carts carrying barbed-wire defences to an advance position where an attack is expected, rolling over the corpses of English and German soldiers who litter the way as they sink into earth that has awaited them. Again there is no sense of difference, in death, between soldiers of either side:

> The plunging limbers over the shattered track
> Racketed with their rusty freight,
> Stuck out like many crowns of thorns,
> And the rusty stakes like sceptres old
> To stay the flood of brutish men
> Upon our brothers dear.
>
> The wheels lurched over sprawled dead
> But pained them not, though their bones crunched,
> Their shut mouths made no moan.
> They lie there huddled, friend and foeman,
> Man born of man, and born of woman,
> And shells go crying over them
> From night till night and now.
>
> Earth has waited for them,
> All the time of their growth
> Fretting for their decay:
> Now she has them at last!
> In the strength of their strength
> Suspended – stopped and held.

The final five stanzas rise to a dramatic and totally unforgettable picture of the advance of the limbers towards men who have only just died, and of one who, still crying out in the last extremities of death, hoping vainly for rescuers, is gone by the time the limbers 'graze his dead face':

A man's brains splattered on
A stretcher-bearer's face;
His shook shoulders slipped their load,
But when they bent to look again
The drowning soul was sunk too deep
For human tenderness.

They left this dead with the older dead,
Stretched at the cross roads.

Burnt black by strange decay
Their sinister faces lie,
The lid over each eye,
The grass and coloured clay
More motion have than they,
Joined to the great sunk silences.

Here is one not long dead;
His dark hearing caught our far wheels,
And the choked soul stretched weak hands
To reach the living word the far wheels said,
The blood-dazed intelligence beating for light,
Crying through the suspense of the far torturing wheels
Swift for the end to break
Or the wheels to break,
Cried as the tide of the world broke over his sight.

Will they come? Will they ever come?
Even as the mixed hoofs of the mules,
The quivering-bellied mules,
And the rushing wheels all mixed
With his tortured upturned sight.
So we crashed round the bend,
We heard his weak scream,
We heard his very last sound,
And our wheels grazed his dead face.

I know of no other poem, even of Owen's, that has such
power in its poetic re-enaction of the reality and the agony
of war.

In the spring of 1915 Rosenberg sent a letter to Marsh which shows that his philosophic and religious views were of a depth and complexity which are not easy for everyone to follow:

If you do find time to read my poems, and I sent them because I think them worth reading, for God's sake! don't say they're obscure. The idea in the poem I like best, 'God Made Blind', I should think is very clear, that we can cheat our malignant fate who has devised a perfect evil for us, by pretending to have as much misery as we can bear, so that it withholds its greater evil, which under the guise of that misery there is secret joy. Love – this joy – burns and grows within us trying to push out to that. Eternity, without us which is God's heart. Joy-love, grows in time too vast to be hidden from God under the guise of gloom. Then we find another way of cheating God. Now through the very joy itself. For by this time we have grown into love, which is the rays of that Eternity of which God is the sun. We have become God Himself. Can God hate and do wrong to Himself?

I think myself the poem is very clear, but if by some foul accident it isn't, I wonder if you see that idea in it?

It is essential, I believe, not to make too much of Rosenberg's Jewish origins and some of his basic ideas, in spite of the importance he attached to, for instance, *Moses*. He stated quite clearly that he wanted to be thought of as an English poet, that is, a poet in the main English tradition, and that ambition he had, in my opinion, achieved by the end of his life cut so short.

7

Jones, Binyon, Gibson, Aldington, Rickword, West and Cameron Wilson

IT is a puzzle for the historian and critic to know where exactly to place David Jones and his *In Parenthesis*, the material 'action' of which takes place between December 1915 and early July 1916 – that is, after the first phase of the Battle of the Somme. Is it prose, a prose poem or poetry? What is remarkable about this most carefully wrought piece of work is the way in which it modulates between what can most easily be read as often highly mannered prose, interspersed with the coarse colloquialisms of army life, to a form that, sometimes by gradations, has the undoubted rhythmic heightening and tension of poetry. For this reason it is not easy to grasp as an artefact at first reading; but there are other reasons for the difficulty a reader is almost certain to find at his first attempt to understand, to judge and to be imaginatively enriched as he certainly will be at the end of the day.

To begin with, the author looks at all wars as one war, as one experience in the history of man. He is much more

concerned with making that connection than with
dwelling on the horrors and pains, the wounds, mutila-
tions, agonized deaths and loss of friends in battle that
every war causes – and that were certainly part of his own
experience. The only exception he is prepared to make to
this view is war as it developed from the later phases of the
Battle of the Somme to the Armistice; though in my
opinion on not altogether consistent grounds. Following
this attitude through, he expects the reader to keep in
mind the wars in the history of England and also their
interpretation in the works of Shakespeare (particularly
Henry V); but above all he expects his reader to know as
much as possible of that shadowy period in our history
between the collapse of the Roman Empire and the
dominance of the Anglo-Saxon invaders. For Jones this is
basically the period of King Arthur as pictured in the
mythical or semi-mythical stories collected and made
into a work of art by Sir Thomas Malory; and the pre-
dominantly Welsh legends that he sees as associated with
that long period lasting over so many centuries.

Another problem is that Jones is liberal with his
explanatory notes and, unless one is already deeply versed
in this literature, a constant reference to them is necessary
on a first and even perhaps on a second reading unless one
has an exceptionally retentive memory. There is also the
further difficulty, for a Protestant, pagan or agnostic
reader, of the continual esoteric references to the rites and
symbols of the Roman Catholic Church, in their most
sacred form.

In Parenthesis is thus far more difficult of access, both
intellectually and imaginatively, than such nevertheless
masterly literary products of the First World War as
Owen's poems, Sassoon's poems and *Memoirs of an Infantry
Officer*, and Graves's *Goodbye To All That*. Whether Jones's
method, inspired as he admits by the overwhelming
experience of reading T. S. Eliot's *The Waste Land* (he

denied having read James Joyce's *Ulysses*), is simply an unique (and perhaps eccentric) phenomenon, or is fertile for the literature of the future, it is still too soon to say.

Jones was born in November 1895, in Kent, and died in 1974. His father, of Welsh stock, was a printer, and his mother, English, came of a family of Thames-side shipbuilders. Thus he came of artisan or craftsman origin on both sides. In spite of his great devotion to Welsh history and Welsh myth, the English tradition was the most important formative influence in his writing. In fact he never learned the Welsh language, and often uses it crudely; and the epigraphs at the beginning of each of the seven parts of *In Parenthesis* are quotations taken from a translation by Edward Anwyl of *Y Godaddin*, the 6th-century Welsh epical poem which commemorates the destruction of a Welsh raiding party of three hundred men by the English at the Battle of Catraeth. It should perhaps be added that there was nothing Cockney about his home surroundings, and that when he uses Cockney slang in the poem it is because, as he says in his Preface, 'as Latin is to the Church, so is Cockney to the Army, no matter what name the regiment bears'. In an admiring review of *In Parenthesis* in *Night and Day* (1937) Evelyn Waugh wrote that it was 'as though Mr. T. S. Eliot had written *The Better 'Ole'*.

Jones's earliest ambition seems to have been to be an artist, and in this he was encouraged by his parents. At the age of fourteen he became a student at the Camberwell School of Art; and it is interesting to note that soon after he was demobilized he sought and obtained a government grant to attend the Westminster School of Art. While he was writing, he was also drawing, painting and engraving. I am convinced that his work as a poet was by no means a 'violin d'Ingres'; his artistic productions may be less regarded by those whose primary interest is in literature; but to me at least both engravings and watercolours come from the same deep and original sources of inspiration as his work with words.

Jones enlisted in the Royal Welch Fusiliers in January 1915, and he stayed as a private soldier with the regiment throughout the war. He was demobilized in December 1918. His division marched towards the Somme in June 1916, and took part in the shattering battle of Mametz Wood. He was wounded, and sent home; he was back in France with his regiment by the end of October 1916. Early in 1918 he had a severe attack of trench fever, and was again sent back to England. When he recovered he was posted to Limerick, and was never in the war zone again.

In Parenthesis occupies itself, in the parts that deal with war, with the period of training in England, the departure for France, in Part Four the night-time advance to the front line ('King Pellam's Launde'), and finally in Part Seven ('The Five Unmistakable Marks', a title taken from Lewis Carroll's 'Hunting of the Snark') with the battle of Mametz Wood. A characteristic example of his method is the following extract from Part Four, where 'Dai Greatcoat' – who is Jones and also can surely be identified with 'John Ball' who is the central character all through – starts his boasting speech. His rhythmic references, as so often in the highlights of the poem, extend beyond the allusions I have mentioned to other mythic and at least partly historical events, and are unlikely to be fully understood without reference to the author's notes:

This Dai adjusts his slipping shoulder-straps, wraps close his misfit outsize greatcoat – he articulates his English with an alien care.

My fathers were with the Black Prinse of Wales
at the passion of
the blind Bohemian king.
They served in these fields,

it is in the histories that you can read it, Corporal – boys
Gower, they were – it is writ down – yes.
   Wot about Methuselum, Taffy?
I was with Abel when his brother found him,
under the green tree.
I built a shit-house for Artaxerxes.
I was the spear in Balin's hand
                that made waste King Pellam's land.

   The same method, modulating from prose to the poetic
and back again, is shown in this passage from Part Seven:

But sweet sister death has gone debauched today and
stalks on this high ground with strumpet confidence,
makes no coy veiling of her appetite but leers from you to
me with all her parts discovered.

By one and one the line gaps, where her fancy will –
                       howsoever
they may howl for their virginity
she holds them – who impinge less on space
sink limply to a heap
nourish a lesser category of being
like those other who fructify the land
like Tristram
Lamorak de Galis
Alisand le Orphelin
Beaumains who was youngest
or all of them in shaft-shade
at strait Thermopylae
or the sweet brothers Balin and Balan
embraced beneath their single monument.
   Jonathan my lovely one
on Gelboe mountain
and the young man Absalom.
White Hart transfixed in his dark lodge.
Peredur of steel arms
and he who with intention took grass of that field to
                       be for him

the Species of Bread.
  Taillefer the maker,
and on the same day,
thirty thousand other ranks.
And in the country of Bearn – Oliver
and all the rest – so many without memento
beneath the tumuli on the high hills
and under the harvest places.

But how intolerably bright the morning is where we who
are alive and remain, walk lifted up, carried forward by an
effective word.

But red horses now – blare every trump without economy,
burn boat and sever every tie every held thing goes west
and tethering snapt, bolts unshot and brass doors flung
wide and you go forward, foot goes another step further.

  More dramatic – and Jones's method rises easily to the
dramatic and realistic but at the same time containing its
allusive references to Shakespeare and to myth – is the
following extract from Part Seven:

Jerry's through on the flank . . . and: Beat it! –
that's what that one said as he ran past:
Bosches back in Strip Trench – it's a
monumental bollocks every time
and but we avoid wisely there is but death.

Lance-Corporal Bains, sweating on the top line, reckoned
he'd clicked a cushy get away; but Captain Cadwaladr
holds the westward ride, & that's torn it for the dodger.
Captain Cadwaladr is come to the breach full of familiar
blasphemies. He wants the senior private – the front is
half-right and what whore's bastard gave the retire and:
Through on the flank my arse.
  Captain Cadwaladr restores
the Excellent Disciplines of the Wars.

And then he might see sometime the battle was driven a bow draught from the castle and sometime it was at the gates of the castle.

Jones began to write *In Parenthesis* slowly and with great difficulty sometime in the mid-1920s, and was still at work at it in 1932. He had joined Eric Gill's community at Ditchling Common in 1921, working as a craftsman and painter. When the split occurred in this Catholic community in 1924, Jones moved to Capel-y-ffin in the Black Mountains in South Wales. *In Parenthesis* was published in June 1937, and was awarded the Hawthornden Prize in 1938. In 1952 he published a sequel, though not to do with his war experiences, *Anathémata*. He says in his Preface:

So what to the question: what is this writing about? I answer that it is about one's own 'thing', which *res* is unavoidably part and parcel of the Western Christian *res*, as intended by and dependent upon his being indigenous to this island.

After the *Anathémata* he published a number of other poems – or prose poems – of the highest distinction, but perhaps of even more arcane reference.

A handful of other survivors also deserve to be mentioned, rather for their later work and in a different sphere than for their contribution to the poetry I have been studying. Laurence Binyon, born in 1869 and therefore already in his mid-forties when war broke out, was present on the Western Front as a Red Cross orderly in 1916. He is more famous for his poem 'For the Fallen' than any others, but that was written, contrary to the general opinion, in September 1914, long before even Brooke's war sonnets had been written. Nevertheless, out of his direct experiences in the Red Cross, he wrote one poem which I find particularly moving, 'Fetching the Wounded'.

Wilfred Gibson, close friend of Brooke and one of the beneficiaries of his will, served in the ranks from 1914, but was only a short time at the Front. His poems celebrated the common fighting soldier, but few of them achieved especial distinction. One short poem, of only eight lines, 'Mark Anderson', has the terse, unsentimental expression of a harrowing episode that must have been the personal experience of many who watched by the death-bed of fellow soldiers and friends wounded in the fighting, and is in contrast to Binyon's more generalized elegiac lines.

Richard Aldington, born in 1892, and badly gassed on the Western Front between 1916 and 1918, is more remembered for his sardonic anti-war prose book, *Death of a Hero*, which made his name, than for his poetry. He was a leading exponent of the Imagist school, but one of his earlier more conventional poems, 'Field Manoeuvres', has an authentic vivid quality that gives it a place of its own.

One other survivor of the war, Edgell Rickword, deserves special mention, not because he contributed more than a small handful of poems to the literature of the war, but because of his later distinction as a highly individual intellectual poet (one thinks especially of 'Invocation to Angels', published in 1928), critic and editor. He was born in 1898, and served in the last stages of the fighting on the Western Front. Some of his poems were published in periodicals at the time and one especially has remained in memory and has appeared in many anthologies of war poetry, 'Winter Warfare'.

Many dozens of books of poetry, by soldiers who were killed in the fighting, were published both before the war ended and after, in addition to those which I have given special consideration in this study. They had cherished value for relations and friends in giving the dead a voice,

but very little remains of significance today, except as a
testimony to the strength of the impulse of the English
soldiers of education (and to a far greater degree it seems
to me than their comparable French allies and German
and Austrian adversaries) to extract what drops of honey
they could from the strange and bitter experience they
so unexpectedly, so unpreparedly, found themselves
enduring. One day hitherto unknown poets of unusual
achievement may be discovered from manuscripts lying in
forgotten archives, though the probability seems small. Of
what we have, in libraries and on second-hand bookstalls,
individual poems can be found in many anthologies,
selected both in the early post-war years and more
recently. Among those that have appealed to me personally I should mention in conclusion Arthur Graeme West's
'God How I Hate You'. West, evidently of exceptional
intelligence, won scholarships to his public school and to
Oxford, and enlisted in the ranks because his imperfect
eyesight prevented him applying for a commission. He
served in France between November 1915 and March
1916. By that time standards of fitness had been relaxed,
and he accepted a commission in September. In April
1917 he was killed by a sniper's bullet.

   Another poet, T. P. Cameron Wilson, was a hitherto
unknown young schoolmaster who joined the Sherwood
Foresters, in which regiment he soon became a captain.
He was killed in action in March 1918. His book of poems,
Magpies in Picardy and Other Poems, was published by Harold
Monro at the Poetry Bookshop, and the title poem has a
certain haunting originality which is not easily forgotten.
The poem appeared in Lord Wavell's *Other Men's Flowers*
in 1944:

> The magpies in Picardy
> Are more than I can tell.
> They flicker down the dusty roads
> And cast a magic spell

On the men who march through Picardy,
Through Picardy to Hell.

(The blackbird flies with panic,
The swallow goes like light,
The finches move like ladies,
The owl floats by at night;
But the great and flashing magpie
He flies as artists might.)

A magpie in Picardy
Told me secret things –
Of the music in white feathers,
And the sunlight that sings
And dances in deep shadows –
He told me with his wings.

(The hawk is cruel and rigid,
He watches from a height;
The rook is slow and sombre,
The robin loves to fight;
But the great and flashing magpie
He flies as lovers might.)

He told me that in Picardy,
An age ago or more,
While all his fathers still were eggs,
These dusty highways bore
Brown singing soldiers marching out
Through Picardy to war.

He said that still through chaos
Works on the ancient plan
And two things have altered not
Since first the world began –
The beauty of the wild green earth
And the bravery of man.

(For the sparrow flies unthinking
And quarrels in his flight;

The heron trails his legs behind,
The lark goes out of sight;
But the great and flashing magpie
He flies as poets might.)

It is perhaps not inappropriate to end my study of the English poets of the First World War with this simple but not untalented poem of Cameron Wilson's, because it has the qualities that appear in so much of the more distinguished poetry of the time: the feeling for nature and community with nature, in the midst of the fighting, in the work of Blunden, Gurney, and even in Grenfell's 'Into Battle', Rosenberg's 'Returning We Hear the Larks' and 'Break of Day in the Trenches', not to mention many other lesser poems; and hints at the underlying conviction, so powerful in Jones, that battle and 'the bravery of man' are phenomena not merely of the First World War but of the conditions of man's existence.

The poetry of the First World War, and particularly the poetry of Owen, Sassoon and Blunden, was widely read by the generation on whom the burden of fighting the Second World War fell. It made the deepest impression on their minds. However, no poems of any distinction in the mood of Brooke and Grenfell were written by Alun Lewis, Keith Douglas, Sidney Keyes or Roy Fuller. This was clearly due to the fact that the origins and conditions of the Second War were so different: England entered the war feeling that the already proven record of their Nazi and Fascist opponents, in terms of international aggression and inhuman attack on their minorities, in particular the Jews in Germany, seemed to make it a just war, if ever a war can be held to be just. This was not the case with the First War as the poetry I have discussed, especially that written after 1916, full of despair and disillusionment, testifies. Nevertheless, I cannot help feeling that Owen's

poem, 'The End', is as relevant to the Second World
War – indeed to all wars – as it is to the First World War:

> After the blast of lightning from the east,
> The flourish of loud clouds, the Chariot Throne;
> After the drums of time have rolled and ceased,
> And by the bronze west long retreat is blown,
>
> Shall Life renew these bodies? Of a truth
> All death will he annul, all tears assuage? –
> Or fill these void veins full again with youth,
> And wash, with an immortal water, Age?
>
> When I do ask white Age he saith not so:
> 'My head hangs weighed with snow.'
> And when I hearken to the Earth, she saith:
> 'My fiery heart shrinks, aching. It is death.
> Mine ancient scars shall not be glorified,
> Nor my titanic tears, the seas, be dried.'

Chronology

1878 Edward Thomas born.
1886 Siegfried Sassoon born.
1887 Rupert Brooke born.
1888 Julian Grenfell born.
　　 F. W. Harvey born.
1890 Ivor Gurney born.
　　 Isaac Rosenberg born.
1892 Osbert Sitwell born.
1893 Wilfred Owen born.
　　 Robert Nichols born.
　　 Herbert Read born.
1895 Robert Graves born.
　　 David Jones born.
　　 Charles Hamilton Sorley born.
1896 Edmund Blunden born.
1911 Rupert Brooke's *Poems 1911* is published in December.
1911–12 *Georgian Poetry*, edited by Edward Marsh, is published.
1912 Osbert Sitwell joins the Grenadier Guards.
1914 England declares war on Germany on 4 August.
　　 Siegfried Sassoon and Charles Sorley enlist in August.
　　 Retreat from Mons on 24 August.
　　 Battle of the Marne (5–15 September).
　　 1st Battle of Ypres (October–November).
　　 Minimum height for recruits is reduced to 5 ft. 3 in., on 5 November.
　　 Rupert Brooke writes 'The Dead', and his *1914 Sonnets* is published in *New Numbers* in December.
　　 Charles Sorley writes 'To Germany', 'When You See Millions of the Mouthless Dead' and 'Route March'.
1915 David Jones enlists in the Royal Welch Fusiliers on 2 January.

Siegfried Sassoon falls from his horse in January and is sent home for two months to recover from a broken arm.

Isaac Rosenberg returns to England from South Africa in February and joins up a few months later.

British offensive at Neuve Chapelle (10–13 March) fails.

2nd Battle of Ypres (April–May) in which Germans first use poison gas as a weapon.

Rupert Brooke writes 'Fragment' soon before he dies on his way to the Gallipoli expedition on 23 April. British troops begin landing at Gallipoli on 25 April.

British offensive at Festubert (9–25 May) fails.

Julian Grenfell writes 'Into Battle'. He dies on 26 May after being wounded in the head by a shell splinter at Ypres.

Edward Thomas enlists in the Artists' Rifles in July.

British offensive at Loos (September–October) fails; their gas is blown back at them. Charles Sorley is killed.

Wilfred Owen joins the Artists' Rifles on 22 October.

Siegfried Sassoon is sent to France with the First Battalion of the Royal Welch Fusiliers, where he soon meets Robert Graves.

Troops withdraw from Gallipoli in December.

Ivor Gurney enlists in the 2nd/5th Gloucesters.

Rupert Brooke's *1914 and Other Poems* is published.

1916 Lord Derby introduces conscription in the Military Service Act, 27 January.

German attack on Verdun in February. This leads in due course to French mutinies.

Isaac Rosenberg is sent to France in May.

Osbert Sitwell's 'Therefore the Name of it is called Babel' is published in May.

Robert Graves writes 'The Last Post' in June, and his *Over the Brazier* is published.

The allies launch Somme offensive on the Western Front on 1 July. Tanks are used for the first time.

Wilfred Owen sails to France, attached to the Lancashire Fusiliers, on 29 December.

F. W. Harvey is taken prisoner and spends the rest of the war in a prisoner-of-war camp.

Charles Sorley's *Marlborough and Other Poems* is published.

Isaac Rosenberg's *Moses* is published.

1917 Battle of Arras (9–14 April). Edward Thomas is killed on 9 April by the blast of a shell.

America enters the war in April.

Edward Thomas's *Poems* is published.

Having been sent to the 13th Casualty Clearing Station in the middle of March, Wilfred Owen returns to his battalion in April. At the beginning of May he is again sent to the Station and to other hospitals. On 18 June he is sent back to England.

Having returned to France in February, Siegfried Sassoon is wounded in the neck in the attack on the Hindenburg defences. *The Old Huntsman* is published in May. In July Sassoon meets Wilfred Owen at Craiglockhart military hospital in Edinburgh, and on 7 July mails his letter of protest against the war to the commanding officer at Litherland. He composes most of the poems for *Counter-Attack*.

Robert Graves is wounded in July, and wrongly posted as 'died of wounds'.

3rd Battle of Ypres (Passchendaele) is waged with high casualties (July–December).

Ivor Gurney is gassed at St Julien on 10 September.

The Russian Revolution takes place (November) and Russia makes a separate peace with Germany.

Robert Graves's *Fairies and Fusiliers* is published in November.

Ivor Gurney's *Severn and Somme* is published.

Robert Nichols's *Ardours and Endurances* is published.

1918 Edward Thomas's *Last Poems* is published.

In February Siegfried Sassoon is sent to Egypt and writes 'I Stood with the Dead'.

Final German offensives on the Western Front from March to July.

Isaac Rosenberg is killed at dawn on 1 April while on night patrol.

Siegfried Sassoon is sent to France in May. He is wounded in the head on 13 July. *Counter-Attack* is published in July.

Wilfred Owen and Osbert Sitwell meet on leave in London in July.

Allied counter-offensive in August, in which the American army takes part in September.

Siegfried Sassoon sees Wilfred Owen for the last time in August. Owen returns to France at the beginning of September. He is awarded the Military Cross on 1 October.

Having attempted suicide, Ivor

Gurney is discharged from the army in October.

Owen is killed while trying to get his men across the Sambre canal on 4 November.

The Armistice is declared on 11 November.

1919 Herbert Read's *Naked Warriors* and *Ecologues* are published.

A selection of Wilfred Owen's poems is published in *Wheels*, 2 November.

1922 Ivor Gurney is admitted to an asylum, Barnwood, near Gloucester, where he spends most of the rest of his life.

Isaac Rosenberg's *Poems* is published.

1925 Herbert Read's *In Retreat* is published.

1928 Edmund Blunden's *Undertones of War* is published.

1929 Robert Graves's *Goodbye To All That* is published (2nd edn 1957).

1930 Siegfried Sassoon's *Memoirs of an Infantry Officer* is published.

Herbert Read's *Ambush* is published.

1933 Herbert Read's *The End of a War* is published.

1937 David Jones's *In Parenthesis* is published.

1940 Herbert Read writes 'To A Conscript of 1940'.

1947 Robert Graves writes 'Recalling War'.

Bibliography

General books consulted

Bernard Bergonzi, *Heroes' Twilight* (Constable 1965)

Joseph Cohen, *Journey to the Trenches* (Robson Books 1975)

W. Cooke, *Edward Thomas* (Faber and Faber 1970)

Walter de la Mare, *Rupert Brooke and the Intellectual Imagination* (Sidgwick and Jackson 1919)

Paul Fussell, *The Great War and Modern Memory* (Oxford University Press 1975)

Christopher Hassall, *Rupert Brooke* (Faber and Faber 1964)

Michael Hurd, *The Ordeal of Ivor Gurney* (Oxford University Press 1978)

John Johnston, *English Poetry of the First World War* (Oxford University Press 1964)

John Lehmann, *Rupert Brooke: His Life and His Legend* (Weidenfeld and Nicolson 1980)

Timothy Rogers, *Rupert Brooke* (Routledge and Kegan Paul 1971)

Jon Stallworthy, *Wilfred Owen* (Oxford University Press 1974)

Helen Thomas, *As it Was – World Without End* (Faber and Faber 1956)

Denis Winter, *Death's Men* (Allen Lane 1978)

Anthologies

Brian Gardner, *Up the Line to Death* (Methuen 1964)

Ian Parsons, *Men Who March Away* (Chatto and Windus 1965)

Jon Silkin, *The Penguin Book of First World War Poetry* (Penguin/Allen Lane 1979)

The Poets

Richard Aldington, *Collected Poems* (Allen Wingate 1948)

Laurence Binyon, *The Four Years* (Elkin Mathews 1919); *Collected Poems* (Macmillan 1931)

Edmund Blunden, *Undertones of War* (Cobden-Sanderson 1928), *Poems 1914–1930* (Cobden-Sanderson 1930)

Rupert Brooke, *Collected Poems*, with memoir by Edward Marsh (Sidgwick and Jackson 1918); *Poetical Works*, ed. Geoffrey Keynes (Faber and Faber 1946, 1974); *Selected Letters*, ed. Geoffrey Keynes (Faber and Faber 1968)

Robert Graves, *Over the Brazier* (The Poetry Bookshop 1916); *Fairies and Fusiliers* (Heinemann 1917); *Goodbye To All That* (Cape 1929; Cassell 1957); *Collected Poems* (Cassell 1938); *Collected Poems 1914–1947* (Cassell 1948)

Ivor Gurney, *Severn and Somme* (Sidgwick and Jackson 1917); *Poems 1890–1937* (Chatto and Windus 1973); a new, definitive edition of Gurney's poems, edited by P. J. Kavanagh, is due presently from Oxford University Press

F. W. Harvey, *Gloucestershire Friends* (Sidgwick and Jackson 1917)

David Jones, *In Parenthesis* (Faber and Faber 1937); *Dai Greatcoat: Selected Letters*, ed. Rene Hague (Faber and Faber 1980)

Robert Nichols, *Ardours and Endurances* (Chatto and Windus 1917); *Such Was My Singing* (Collins 1942)

Wilfred Owen, *Poems*, introduction by Siegfried Sassoon (Chatto and Windus 1920); *Collected Poems*, ed. C. Day Lewis (Chatto and Windus 1963); *Collected Letters* (Oxford University Press 1968)

Herbert Read, *Naked Warriors* (Art and Letters 1919); *Ecologues* (Westminster: Cyril W. Beaumont 1919); *In Retreat* (L. and V. Woolf 1925); *Collected Poems* (Faber and Gwyer 1926); *The End of a War* (Faber and Faber 1933); *Collected Poems* and *The Contrary Experience* (Faber and Faber 1963)

Edgell Rickword, *Behind The Eyes* (Sidgwick and Jackson 1921); *Collected Poems* (Carcanet 1976)

Isaac Rosenberg, *Moses* (Paraga Printing Works 1916); *Poems* (Heinemann 1922); *Collected Works*, ed. Ian Parsons (Chatto and Windus 1979)

Siegfried Sassoon, *The Old Huntsman* (Heinemann 1917); *The Complete Memoirs of George Sherston* (Memoirs of a Fox-hunting Man, Memoirs of an Infantry Officer and Sherston's Progress) (Faber and Faber 1937); *The Weald of Youth* (Faber and Faber 1942); *Siegfried's Journey* (Faber and Faber 1945); *Collected Poems* (Faber and Faber 1947)

Osbert Sitwell, *Selected Poems* (Duckworth 1943); *Left Hand, Right Hand* (Macmillan 1945)

Charles Hamilton Sorley, *Marlborough and Other Poems, Letters from Germany*, and *The Letters, with a Chapter of Biography* (Cambridge University Press 1916)

Edward Thomas, *Collected Poems* ed. R. George Thomas (Oxford University Press 1978, 1981)

Arthur Graeme West, *The Diary of a Dead Officer* (Allen and Unwin 1918)

T. P. Cameron Wilson, *Magpies in Picardy and Other Poems* (The Poetry Bookshop 1919)

List of Illustrations

Text Illustrations: numbers refer to pages

published by the Parliamentary Recruiting Committee. Imperial War Museum, London

53 A letter from Siegfried Sassoon to Robert Ross, written from Craiglockhart military hospital, July 1917. Imperial War Museum, London

63 Adrian Hill, *Gavrelle Trench*, 1917. Ink and wash, 14 × 20¼ (35.6 × 51.4). Imperial War Museum, London

71 Muirhead Bone, *Deniécourt Château, Estrées*, May 1917. Charcoal, 22 × 30 (55.9 × 76.2). Imperial War Museum, London

87 John Nash, a study for *A French Highway*, c. 1918. Pen and pencil, 7½ × 10 (19 × 25.4). Imperial War Museum, London

107 Blair Hughes-Stanton, interior of a hospital ward. Wood-engraving, 3²/₃ × 5 (9.3 × 12.7), executed for Velona Pilcher, *The Searcher*, a war play, 1929. Courtesy of Blair Hughes-Stanton

121 Adrian Hill, detail from *A Stretcher Party, a German prisoner assists*. Ink and wash, 10¼ × 18½ (26 × 47). Imperial War Museum, London

125 Adrian Hill, *The Completed Strong Point, on the Ridge, Ypres*. Ink and wash, 12¾ × 18 (32.4 × 45.7). Imperial War Museum, London

136 Blair Hughes-Stanton, graveyard. Detail from a wood-engraving, 3²/₃ × 5 (9.3 × 12.7), executed for Velona Pilcher, *The Searcher*, a war play, 1929. Courtesy of Blair Hughes-Stanton

Plates

1 'Your Country's Call . . .'. Poster published by the Parliamentary Recruiting Committee, c. 1915. Imperial War Museum, London

2 Julian Henry Francis Grenfell, c. 1914. BBC Hulton Picture Library

3 Rupert Brooke, 1913. Photo Sherill Schell. By permission of the Literary Trustees of Rupert Brooke and of King's College Library, Cambridge

4 Charles Hamilton Sorley. Portrait by C. Jameson, 1916. Chalk, 18 × 13¾ (46 × 35.2). National Portrait Gallery, London

5 Robert Nichols. Portrait by Augustus John, 1921. Chalk, 12 × 19½ (30.5 × 49.5). National Portrait Gallery, London

6 Rupert Brooke on a picnic with friends, c. 1909. By permission of the Literary Trustees of Rupert Brooke and of King's College Library, Cambridge

7 8th Battalion, Winnipeg Rifles, on Salisbury Plain. Bayonet practice with bags of straw. The Public Archives of Canada

8 Recruits with sergeant. Imperial War Museum, London

9 Measuring recruits with kit. Imperial War Museum, London

10 Augustus John, *Fraternity*, undated. Oil on canvas (unfinished), 93½ × 57 (237.5 × 144.8). Imperial War Museum, London

11 'The Tank . . .'. Poster published by a private company, 1918. Imperial War Museum, London

12 Siegfried Sassoon, 1915. BBC Hulton Picture Library. Photo Imperial War Museum

13 Wilfred Owen, 1916. Trustees of the Harold Owen Estate. Photo Imperial War Museum, London

14 'The Only Road for an Englishman . . .'. Poster published by Johnson Riddle & Co. Ltd. Imperial War Museum, London

15 British troops crossing the River Somme at Brie, near Peronne,

March 1917. Imperial War Museum, London

16 Battle of Passchendaele, August 1917. 18 pounder in the mud. Imperial War Museum, London

17 C. R. W. Nevinson, *La Mitrailleuse*, 1915. Oil on canvas, 24 × 20 (61 × 51). Tate Gallery, London

18 Sentry in a trench looking through a box periscope. Opposite Messines near Ploegsteert Wood, January 1917. Imperial War Museum, London

19 Barbed wire gate. Front-line trench at Cambrin, September 1917. Imperial War Museum, London

20 Stretcher bearers and wounded at a dressing station at Pilckem, July 1917. Imperial War Museum, London

21 Battle of Tardenois. The advance through the Bois du Petit Champ, July 1918. Imperial War Museum, London

22 An advance dressing station on the Montauban-Guillemont Road, September 1916. Imperial War Museum, London

23 A group of officers with Edmund Blunden bottom right, *c.* 1917. Courtesy of Mrs Claire Blunden. Photo Imperial War Museum

24 Edward Thomas with Mervyn, 1900. Courtesy of Mrs Myfannwy Thomas. Photo Imperial War Museum

25 Robert Graves, 1941. BBC Hulton Picture Library

26 Ivor Gurney, 1915. Gloucestershire County Library and by permission of his executor

27 Shell bursting among barbed wire on the battlefield of Beaumont Hamel, December 1916. Imperial War Museum, London

28 The remains of the Menin Road, near Gheluvelt, during the Battle of Ypres, September 1916. Imperial War Museum, London

29 Paul Nash, *Wire*, 1918–19. Ink, pastel and watercolour, 18¾ × 24½ (47.6 × 62.2). Imperial War Museum, London

30 Paul Nash, *The Ypres Salient at Night*, 1918. Oil on canvas, 28 × 36 (71 × 91.4). Imperial War Museum, London

31 C. R. W. Nevinson, *The Harvest of Battle*, 1919. Oil on canvas, 72 × 125 (182.9 × 317.5). Imperial War Museum, London

32 Adrian Hill, *Road Menders*, *c.* 1917. Ink and watercolour, 14½ × 20¾ (36.8 × 52.7). Imperial War Museum, London

33 Sir William Orpen, *Dead Germans in a Trench*, *c.* 1919. Oil on canvas, 36 × 30 (91.4 × 76.2). Imperial War Museum, London

34 Isaac Rosenberg, 1917. Courtesy of the Literary Executors of Isaac Rosenberg. Photo Imperial War Museum, London

35 Isaac Rosenberg. Courtesy of the Literary Executors of Isaac Rosenberg. Photo Imperial War Museum, London

36 Paul Nash, *Existence*, undated. Black chalk and watercolour on brown paper, 19 × 12¾ (48.3 × 32.4). Imperial War Museum, London

37 David Jones, scene in the trenches, undated. Pen and ink drawing, 12 × 8 (30.5 × 20.3). Copyright and reproduced by permission of the Trustees of the David Jones Estate

38 David Jones, 'Huts, Winnal Down, Winchester, Oct. 26th 1915'. Pencil drawing, 8²/3 × 5 ²/3 (22 × 14.4). Copyright and reproduced by permission of the Trustees of the David Jones Estate

39 David Jones, soldier in a trench,

Index

Page numbers in italics refer to illustrations